FEAR
IS THE
MIND
KILLER

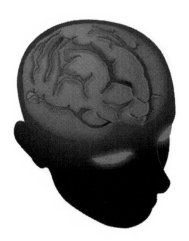

Dennis Allyn

Please check out our website at www.fearisthemindkiller.net

authorHOUSE®

AuthorHouse™
1663 Liberty Drive
Bloomington, IN 47403
www.authorhouse.com
Phone: 1-800-839-8640

First published by AuthorHouse4/28/2009

ISBN: 978-1-4389-7154-4 (sc)
ISBN: 978-1-4389-7153-7 (hc)

Printed in the United States of America
Bloomington, Indiana

This book is printed on acid-free paper.

Dedication

I have given much thought to this as so many have contributed positively towards my development as a human being; as a friend, a father, a son, a brother. My family certainly deserves my thanks. Special thanks go to my mother, who got me started on a search for growth as a person; spiritually, physically, and mentally. Thanks mom, for your example on how to search for the better person within. As I write this my mom is 85 years old and still going strong in her personal growth program as well as her physical exercise regimen. My brother Dale also deserves special thanks as a mentor in my career and a tremendous boost when I was at a time of spiritual and mental crisis. He helped me get on the path to financial security when he helped me gain an interview with a major healthcare sales company many years ago; this at a time when I was struggling financially and somewhat floundering in my sales career. When that company went through a major restructuring and offered me a fork in the road (as Yogi Berra said, "when life gives you a fork in the road, take it"), he helped arrange an interview for me with its major competitor, a choice that turned out extremely well for my career. Special thanks also go to my lovely wife, Liz. I never could have succeeded at anything in my adult life without her loving support and always positive voice and encouragement. Thanks again, to my family, and many friends who have aided me at times of struggle and times of joy. I could never have written this book without your love and support.

TABLE OF CONTENTS

INTRODUCTION

I must not fear. Fear is the mind killer. Fear is the little death that brings total obliteration. Paul Atreides. Dune

"I sense much fear in him. To the dark side, fear leads. Fear leads to anger, anger leads to hate, hate leads to suffering." Yoda, Jedi Master. Star Wars, The Phantom Menace.

"One definition of fear is: Fantasy Experience Appearing Real." Zig Ziglar

"There is no fear in love, but perfect love throws fear outside, because fear exercises a restraint. Indeed, he that is under fear has not been made perfect in love." John. Bible.

"It is impossible to hold a negative emotion and a positive emotion at the same time. To eliminate fear from our lives we must eliminate negative emotions and replace them with positive emotions." Dennis Allyn. *Fear is the Mind Killer.*

I f you understand all you have just read, then you may not need to read this book. But, if any of the above intrigues or confuses you, this book may change your life. In the pages that follow we will explore what fear really is, the types of fear, how it begins in our lives, how to use it to our advantage, and how to eliminate destructive fears. We will explore case studies of homeless people who have let fear take control of them, and contrast this with others who have achieved remarkable things in spite of—and in some cases because of—severe problems or disabilities.

Have you ever wondered why some people with very ordinary skills accomplish extraordinary things and others with above average talents become totally mired down by life's challenges? Some would like to dismiss it as good luck vs. bad luck. But in the vast majority of cases luck has very little to do with it. In fact, we'll explore many that have been very lucky and have led miserable lives, and others who have been dealt very bad hands but have achieved a degree of happiness many only dream of. We can all site examples of wealthy, talented, and privileged people who have made a mess of their lives. Marilyn Monroe, Freddy Prinze, John Bulushi, Jim Morrison, and Kurt Cobain come readily to mind. Others such as Christopher Reeves managed to live very positive lives in spite of terrible infirmities.

What is the difference? Perception. Karen Carpenter (of the Carpenters singing duo) died of anorexia. She perceived herself as fat in spite of the fact she was starving herself to death. Clearly her perception was much different from the reality. When she looked in the mirror she saw a fat person, where everyone around her saw a person who desperately needed food. Karen had money, fame, and legions of fans but she wasn't happy. What fears were her mind killers? Your own mind killers limit you, the reader of this book. They may be small fears or big ones. They may be a wind-drag on an otherwise sleek racecar, or they may be so overwhelming that the brakes of your mind won't allow you to leave the house. Whatever they are, this book can help you overcome, conquer, and eliminate them from your life forever.

CHAPTER ONE

THE JOURNEY

C ome with me on a journey. It isn't a very long journey when compared to your life as a whole. In fact, it is a very short one. But, it may be the most exciting, most revealing, most fulfilling, and ultimately the most important journey you will ever take. Come with me on a journey to the center of your mind. For the next thirty days we—you and I—will explore the most fundamental truths of what makes you, you. What makes you happy, and what makes you sad. What makes you feel good about yourself and what makes you feel less than worthy. What makes you do the things you do? Very few people ever take this journey. I am not merely talking here about people who take a journey to understanding themselves with me, but everyone worldwide for all types of literature in this genre of human behavior. You are a very special person.

First of all, you must understand that you are special just by your very existence. I would like you to spend the time right now widening your focus of who and what you are. If you haven't taken the time to think about these things before, this may be very enlightening for you. Think with me for a moment about the universe and your special place in it. Have you ever spent the time looking up at the starlit sky on a clear night and just pondered the universe? If you haven't done this recently you may want to. Get away somehow from the light of the city, lie on your back, and just look at the wonder of the stars. You can't count them, can you? Scientists have tried to count them and have given up, believing the number to be in the many trillions. Whether you believe in God, or any supreme being/beings for that matter, or whether you believe that everything

1

merely happened by chance, it truly is a marvel, isn't it? Awesome, in fact. Scientists know that the earth is an extremely rare place. In a universe made up of what is estimated to be between 50 billion to 125 billion galaxies, each galaxy with up to 100's of billions of stars, there is only one star—our sun—which scientists have positively identified as having multiple planets in orbit around it. Scientists are virtually positive that only the earth out of the eight planets in our solar system can support life—any kind of life. Astronauts who have left the earth's atmosphere all report that the earth literally looks like a jewel hanging in space. And, out of the incredible abundance of life on the earth—possibly the only life in the universe—you are the most advanced.

It may seem to you sometimes that you are pretty insignificant. I don't know where you live, but especially if you live in a large city with the hustle and bustle of what many times seems like way too many other people, you may not feel very special. But you are. Even if you live in a small town it may seem to you sometimes that you barely exist. The earth only has about six billion humans on it, and though I agree with you that it seems like too many sometimes, if you widen your focus and think about the entire universe, life, and especially human beings, are extremely rare. You on the other hand are even rarer. You are part of a group of people that statistics show is less than 10% of the people on this planet. Less than 1 out of 10 people ever takes the time throughout the entire course of their lives to even try to understand what makes them do the things they do, feel the way they feel, or much less endeavor to try to change these things. The vast majority—more than 9 out of every 10—just muddle through their lives believing, or maybe just accepting, that whatever happens to them is fate, happenstance, or totally beyond their control. You, on the other hand, may realize that you can control your thoughts, what you believe about yourself, how you perceive the world around you, and how you react to the events in that world. In other words, you—not anyone else—control your destiny. The beginning of this control starts with your own mind.

A Jewel in the Universe?

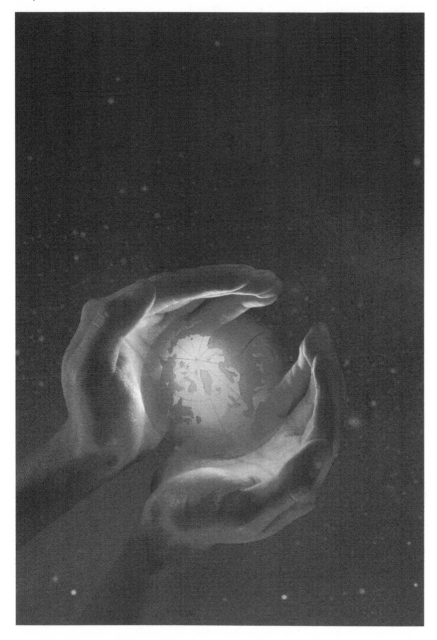

Hopefully, you agree that you as a human being are one of the greatest achievements of the universe—whether by creation of God, or some accidental and incredible interaction of elements. And the most incredible, most amazing part of you is your mind—your human brain. Zig Ziglar is famous for saying, "You are what you feed your mind." Would you agree with that statement? For the next thirty days your mind will become the battlefield on which we will wage the war against doubt, fear, anxiety, and other destructive negative emotions which may have controlled and limited you to various degrees throughout your life. Most people understand that their bodies need to be trained and exercised to function at optimum potential, but how many ever exercise their minds? Today begins an adventure possibly unprecedented in your life. Take the time now to write down the date. Today's date is *Nov 20 2018*. Over the next thirty days you will be asked to read one chapter per day. Since this is your book, you can, of course, read as much as you like. But, you will also be asked to complete an exercise at the end of each chapter. I believe that your greatest success at achieving all you want to become will happen when you complete all the exercises. You must understand that the success you will have from this program comes from you, not from me. Don't misunderstand what I'm saying here; I have total confidence in the methodology and psychological power of every chapter and exercise contained herein. The science contained herein is the most advanced available in the realm of human behavior. Everything in this book has been validated Psychologically, Physiologically, and Spiritually. But, changing your life and all the bad and destructive habits that you may have allowed to shape your life thus far will most likely not be changed by just reading this book. This is not to say that just reading the book has no value—just the opposite is true. However, if you commit to this process as a thirty day life changing exercise where you faithfully complete all the exercises you will most likely notice huge positive changes in the way you view yourself and the direction your life is taking.

You've likely heard the saying, "A journey of a thousand miles starts with the first step." Our journey is one of only thirty days, but the habits you will learn will be habits I believe you will want to carry with you for the rest of your life. Some of the exercises I will ask you to do will be relatively easy—in fact we'll start with a very easy one. Don't worry, they'll get tougher as we go along. Some will take longer than others, but your greatest success will happen when you complete them all. Over the next thirty days you will become aware that some major changes are taking place in your life. You will most likely want to write them down as you notice them. This book is yours and yours alone—keep it as a permanent record of the person you are today and of the person you are becoming as you make the necessary changes to release your inner power. There are blank pages at the end of each chapter for completion of the exercises and also for the recording of the changes you notice about yourself. If you take the time to record these changes, I believe you'll be glad you did. A year, and years from now, this book will still be with you, faithfully standing on your bookshelf or lying in your dresser drawer. You can read it again, or just smile to yourself appreciatively as you read your own-recorded discoveries as you noticed the changes in your viewpoint of yourself and the world around you. You can have the privilege of retrospectively appraising your life and knowing what a better and happier person you've become since today—the date you just recorded above. They say that hindsight is 20/20. Isn't it exciting to know that your vision of your past will be crystal clear as you reflect back on your life from that future time? I believe there will be no doubt of the growth and development you've been able to achieve in your life. Congratulations for taking the first step of buying this book. Congratulations for being the very special person you are, and of taking the challenge of making your life all it is capable of being.

Here's your first exercise: In the space below or in your own notebook write down—as complete as you can—the reasons you bought this book and what you expect to achieve from going through the thirty day program. I want you to think big. After all, if these are your dreams, why not make them great dreams. Make believe that I am a Genie that can grant your wishes—not just three, but as many as you make. The list can be as long as you want it to be, but please take the time right now to dream your biggest dreams. Make believe that this Genie will only grant your wishes if you take the time to write them down. Remember, the more you ask for, the more you will receive. Let your mind run free—don't limit yourself. Have fun. I'll see you tomorrow.

I want to be happy

I don't want to feel like a loser.

I want to be disciplined enough to ~~exercise~~ exercise & run in marathons, bike trips with grandkids

I want to be a great example for my grandchildren & my family.

I was to be loving to everyone. & stop being bitter about loss.

I want to be very financially successful & never a burden to my kids.

I don't want to think of Dave/Susy with such anger I don't want to think about them at all.

I want to be in the best shape - physically, mentally & spiritually of my life!

I want to lose wgt & eat healthy.

I want to be so satisfied & happy with my life that I find it pleasing to be alone or to be with someone.

I want to stop abusing alcohol!

I want to stop feeling guilty about Randy's death.

I want to write a best selling book or screen play.

I want to have strong happy healthy relationships with my family (ALL) & my friends (ALL)

I want to be a better friend.

I want to have a active life full of love & happiness & someone to share some of it with.

I want to meditate more & do yoga.

I want to do photography & or painting

CHAPTER TWO

WHY THE TITLE? —
FEAR IS THE MIND KILLER

Welcome to chapter two. Did you take the time to complete the exercise in chapter one? If you didn't, please go back and do it now before you continue. It is my personal mission through these pages to give you the methods of becoming all you want to become. This requires taking your mind on a road it may not have traveled before. Writing down your desires—your dreams—is the first step on this journey. You and I cannot hope to reach your desired destination without knowing very clearly what that destination is, wouldn't you agree? If you did yesterday's exercise please take the time now to turn back and review your dreams—your new future, if you will. As you continue with me on this journey I believe it will become crystal clear to you that the more vivid your vision of your desired future, the quicker you will arrive there. If you don't yet believe me, then just humor me. I believe you'll be glad you did.

YOUR WISHES HAVE BEEN GRANTED!

It occurred to me yesterday in a conversation with my wife that many who hear of this book, buy it, or receive it as a gift may not understand the significance of the title. Clearly, the implication is that fear kills the mind—but why, and how? You may not even be aware at a conscious level that your life—good or bad—is the sum total of your fears, or lack of fears. There is a wide range of emotions that make up fear. One definition of fear is "The feeling that danger or evil is near." Another definition is "An uneasy feeling, an anxious thought; concern." Terror and dread are types of fear as well, aren't they? We see here a wide scope of intensities of emotion which all fall under the one word—fear. Doubt is very closely aligned with fear, isn't it? Doubt is "An unsettled state of opinion, or a matter of uncertainty." The following short list of different types of fears may make it clearer in your mind as to why I have chosen the title for this book—a book on personal growth and development.

Fear of the dark
Fear of spiders
Fear of failure

Fear of rejection
Fear of success
Fear of heights
Fear of reprisal
Fear of change
Fear of the unknown

All of these fears can cause you to act in a certain way, can't they? If you're afraid of the dark, you try to avoid the dark, don't you? Maybe you leave the light on at night, or maybe you refuse to go upstairs at night until someone turns the light on for you, or goes with you and then turns on the light. Fear of rejection may cause you to not approach someone who you might really want to meet. Or, it may cause you to keep a relationship you really want to grow stronger on a very casual basis. It could be a superior at work, a member of the opposite sex, someone you have a crush on, someone you admire—anyone. Fear of failure may cause you to avoid trying something new, which you feel you might like to try. Or cause you to avoid trying something that could very well improve the quality of your life. Fear of success is an interesting one. Why would anyone fear success? —You may ask. This fear may cause more people—or at least as many—from striving to be more than they already are as fear of failure does. It's closely aligned with "fear of change," and "fear of the unknown." It's an interesting fact about humans that we develop a comfort zone—a little circle of security—around us that we don't want to venture out beyond. No matter how unhappy we may be with our lives we become strangely comfortable with it. You may have friends or relatives who you believe have the potential for much greater happiness and success than what they have, but they just won't venture outside their own little circle of comfort. Are they afraid of making new friends, or maybe they're afraid of losing the ones they have? Are they just afraid of the unknown? Are they afraid they might be perceived as greedy or materialistic?

Behavioral scientists know that everything we as human beings do—every behavior—is caused by the desire to gain pleasure, or the desire to avoid pain. There has been, and continues to be heated debate as to which of these is stronger. Actually, there is probably no right or wrong answer here as it depends on the person. The point is this: Your fears—desire to avoid pain—cause you to avoid circumstances which might cause you pain. Pain is not necessarily physical—although it certainly can be. Emotional distress, anxiety, nervousness, stress, can all be more devastating in their effects on your behavior than the desire to avoid physical pain. Of course, all these mental pains can manifest themselves in physical pain as well. Ulcers, dizzy spells, heart attack, back pain, stiff neck, headache, and many other physical manifestations can be directly caused by mental anguish.

If your expectation of pleasure is greater than your expectation of pain you will move towards something. If the reverse is true you will move away from it. Every single action in your life can be boiled down to this simple truth. Wouldn't you agree that as far as fear is concerned, to gain the most pleasure and joy you are capable of gaining, it is up to you to make sure that your fears are all rational fears, not irrational ones? Rational fears are fears that empower you, irrational fears are those which limit your development and growth. I have a fear that if I step in front of a moving semi I'll be much the worse for it. I think you'll agree that is a rational fear. But, if I so fear stepping in front of a moving semi that I won't venture out of my home, that is an irrational fear. It is your challenge—if you strive to be more than you are—to make sure that all your fears are rational ones.

As we'll explore in great detail as you read further on in this book, your fears are based on your expectations of an outcome. If you expect positive results—you believe it in your heart—you will have no fear will you? If you expect negative results, you will have fear, wouldn't you agree? It's that simple, isn't it? My goal is for you to learn how to change your expectation of events so that instead of fearing a negative outcome, you will look forward to the future knowing that positive outcomes await you. A fundamental truth of human behavior is that we feel good about ourselves to the exact degree that we feel in control of our own lives. You will most likely gain further appreciation of this truth as we continue on our journey. When you learn how to manage your expectations of any event you are now in control. Your fears, doubts, anxieties, and all the other negative emotions that attach themselves to these—like flypaper— will no longer control you. Flypaper is a strip of paper with sticky glue and a scent that attracts flies, which is designed to hang from the ceiling. Strips of flypaper used to hang from the ceilings in restaurants and factories. The theory was that if the flies went to the flypaper—and ultimately stuck to it and died—they would not be flying around you and your food. It certainly wasn't too pretty to look at, but it did tend to reduce the fly population in the restaurant. Through the steps we will take together in this book the glue on the flypaper of your negative thoughts will get less and less sticky, until finally it won't stick at all.

You will learn that in order to control your destiny, and have the peace of mind that you need, want, and deserve you must take responsibility for every event in your life. This is a good thing, not something to fear. You will learn how to manage your state of mind, or what behavioral scientists call your mental states. When you do, your anxieties will melt away. You will learn how to expect the best for yourself every day of your life. When you have mastered these techniques you will be the one who truly controls your destiny. Believe it or not, you've already made great progress. Congratulations.

The title for this book comes from a book written by Frank Herbert, which was originally copyrighted in 1965. The book is *Dune*. It's a classic science fiction book. Whether you like science fiction or not this reference for fear will hopefully make an impact on your understanding of how to look at your own fears. Paul Atreides, the Duke's son, had to undergo a test to determine if he was a human. He had to put his right hand into a black box and not pull it out of the box until permitted. A sharp needle containing a deadly poison was placed against his neck. If he pulled his hand out of the box before being allowed, the needle would pierce his neck and he would die. He was told only that the box contained pain, nothing else.

It started with a gentle tingling—*Not too bad*, he thought. The tingling became an itch—*This is easy*, and then he could feel warmth, then heat, then burning, until soon he felt his flesh melting from his hand. The pain was excruciating, and yet if he withdrew his hand from the box he would die. As the son of the Duke Atreides, Paul had undergone rigorous training in the Bene Gessirit disciplines, including intense mental rigors. The Bene Gessirits taught the individual to say this to himself when faced with great fear: *I must not fear. Fear is the mind-killer. Fear is the little death that brings total obliteration. I will face my fear. I will permit it to pass over me and through me. And when it has gone past I will turn the inner eye to see its path. Where the fear has gone there will be nothing. Only I will remain.* The pain Paul experienced was unbearable, and yet finally it was gone. When allowed to take his hand from the box he hesitated even to look at it, and yet there was no damage at all. The pain was caused from nerve induction, leaving no permanent damage of any kind.

Much can be learned from this, I feel. I hope you agree that when we allow our fears to limit us from being all we are capable of being we rob ourselves of some of our life's joy and value. This is a "little death." Notice that Paul passed his test by focusing on a positive future, not the pain, and certainly not his fear. You and I can do the same thing. All it requires is the understanding of what fear is, and some simple steps, which anyone—including you—can learn.

Your assignment for today will be a lot of fun for you. It is the first time—but not the last—that you will use visualization techniques to re-program your subconscious mind. Much of the programming that makes up the you of today has happened without you planning it. Because of that, much of it is negative. Remember that we move toward events that we expect pleasure from, and we move away from events we anticipate pain from. These visualizations will help to program your subconscious mind, which controls your behavior every day without your conscious awareness of it, to expect positive outcomes—pleasure. Yesterday you made a list of what you expect to gain from reading this book. I hope your list is an extensive one. I also hope your expectations of what you want to gain from this program are great ones. You should have at least ten things that you expect to gain.

LET YOURSELF DREAM BIG DREAMS

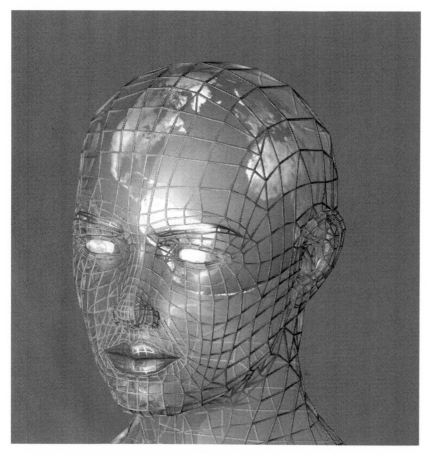

Now, I would like you to write down how you'll feel when all these things are realized. Remember that I am the Genie that can grant your ten wishes. Your wishes have been granted. Let your mind run free with no reigns at all—nothing to hold you back.

Change occurs when our expectation of pleasure by making a change becomes greater than our fear of the pain of change. It can be stated this way: Change = (pain of present>pain of change) + clear vision + first step towards the future. Another way to say this is change = desperation + aspiration + perspiration. Or, the greater the benefits of your new future the quicker the change happens. For each of the ten expectations you wrote down make a list of at least five benefits—positive feelings you and/or others will gain from it.

[handwritten notes in margin]
Happiness = health, love, energy, satisfaction
Discipline = health, happiness, exercising, good shape
Great Example = disciplined, creative financial secure

Is the list complete? Good. Now I would like you to close your eyes and visualize how your life has changed as a result of these ten expectations having been met. The key here is to completely relax— don't force your mind, relax it. Allow your mind to form as complete a visualization of what your life—what you—will be like a year from now without any fear or doubts. All your expectations have come true. Your ten wishes have been granted completely. What are the pictures that you see? What sounds do you hear? Are there people with you? Who are they? How happy are their faces? What does your future smell like? Are there tastes? If so, what do they taste like?

Now, visualize your future five years from now. Once again, let your mind relax and give you the mental pictures. What are the colors? How do you feel about yourself now that you have no fears at all?

Ten years:

Twenty years:

Just as in all the exercises in this book, the greater your commitment to doing them the greater the success. Do you like what you see? Great! Tomorrow will be even better. Have fun, and I'll see you then.

CHAPTER THREE

THE LIMITS YOU PLACE ON YOURSELF

D id you do your visualization exercises yesterday? I hope you took yourself to a quiet place and let your mind completely relax as you formed clear and perfect visualizations of your new future. If you did, you are already well on your way there. If you didn't, please take the time to do it now. Remember that if you keep on doing what you've always done, you'll keep on getting what you've always gotten. I presume you're reading this book because you want to make some changes. Doing the exercises is most likely the only way your mind will accept the future you desire. Not doing them will most likely give you a future similar to your past. Visualizations extend the boundaries of your self-beliefs. Without your conscious awareness of it, you begin to believe that you are capable of much greater accomplishments. Your subconscious "ceiling of limitations" has been significantly raised.

Dennis Allyn

WHAT CAN YOU LEARN FROM A FLEA?

Are you operating within self-imposed limitations? Most likely you are. You see; your past has trained you to look at yourself a certain way, and the way you view yourself is the filter through which you interpret every event in your life. In your quest to be all you can become you must first realize how you perceive your limitations today.

When you think of a flea what is the first thing that comes to your mind? Sure, they're small, they bite, they infest dogs and cats, they're hard to kill, etc. But, for most people the first thing they think of is the amazing jumping power of this tiny creature. Have you ever tried to catch a flea? Did you know that if you had the jumping power of the flea that you could literally jump over the Empire State Building? A flea doesn't have to be trained to jump, does it? Instinctively this amazing insect jumps whenever it's threatened in any way. You may not be aware that fleas can actually be trained to do tricks like walk a tight rope, pull a cart, run a treadmill and other curiosities. There really are flea circuses where these miniature Charles Atlases perform amazing feats of strength—without jumping. When I heard of flea circuses I wondered how a flea could be trained not to jump. You may find it interesting that all they do is put them in a jar with

16

a top on a few inches above the bottom. Every time the flea jumps it hits its head on the ceiling. Over and over again the flea jumps, but before too long the flea realizes that jumping takes it nowhere. Maybe it also realizes in its little flea brain that it hurts its head every time it tries to jump so eventually it stops trying. The interesting thing about this training is that once the flea stops jumping the top can be removed, the flea can be taken from the jar, and it will never jump again. It will only crawl for the rest of its life—until finally, it dies. Since the flea is so powerful for its size it can actually pull a cart weighing hundreds of times its own weight, but it will never ever jump again.

IF YOU HAD THE JUMPING POWER OF THE FLEA.....

Think about that for a minute. A creature whose every instinct is to use its incredible talent in a certain way can be permanently re-programmed just that easily to never use its natural abilities again.

How much are you like that flea? How much of your natural ability is being wasted—maybe forever—because of the limitations your mind has accepted for you. You may be thinking, "How stupid of that flea. Doesn't it ever realize that the top is no longer there? Why doesn't it try again?" Well, what about you? Believe it or not, you are still performing within the artificial limitations placed on you by your perception of the big bad world from when you were a very small child. Without you being consciously aware of it, every single act in your life is accomplished within the limits of your beliefs about yourself. Your perception of everything around you is based on your internal belief system. Just as that flea believes that the limitation of that ceiling is always there, you have placed limitations on yourself which will remain forever—until you die—unless you take the conscious steps of removing them. Would you like to remove these artificial limitations from your belief system? Would you like to be all that you're capable of being? Would you like to utilize the gifts that you have for the benefit of others and yourself?

WILL *YOU* EVER JUMP AGAIN?

If you're not convinced yet that your perception of the world is unique to you, look at the picture on the opposite page. What do you see? Go ahead and look at the picture before you keep reading. Don't cheat and read ahead or you'll miss the point. Don't worry; I'll wait.

18

EDITING ALLOWS IN ONLY THAT DATA CONSISTENT WITH YOUR INTERNAL BELIEFS AND FILTERS OUT ALL THAT DOESN'T FIT.

It may interest you to know that if you were in a room of 100 people, fifty or so would see a picture of a beautiful, aristocratic young woman, and fifty or so would see a picture of an old ugly hag. There's no right or wrong answer here, but the point is that we see things in a certain way based on our past experiences and what perception filters we use to interpret the world around us. Police detectives, insurance investigators, and others who question witnesses of particular events often hear almost completely different stories from those who viewed what should essentially be the same thing. Why? The psychological term for this process is "editing." Our minds edit out information based on the perception filter of our experience and self-image, allowing in only the information which is deemed relevant to our own internal belief system. You know doubt have heard of the Rorschach test where different people see different things when shown a series of inkblots. Have you ever left a movie thinking to yourself how awful it was and been surprised to find that a friend who watched it with you absolutely loved it? You may have wondered if they saw the same movie you did. Or, have you ever left a party thinking that it was the most boring party you'd ever been to, only to find that your friend/friends totally enjoyed themselves? These events aren't merely a matter of personal taste, but actually can be attributed to how our minds perceive the world around us. You no doubt have heard the saying; "Perception is reality." Your perception is your reality, isn't it? Do you like the reality of your life? If not, could it be that your perception of yourself needs to change? Are you the flea with a ceiling over your head that isn't even there?

Take a look at the picture again. If you saw the young woman I would like you to now look at her ear. Instead of looking at an ear try to see an eye of an old woman with the chin of your young woman now the nose of the old hag. What was the necklace of your young lady is now the partially open mouth of the old hag. If you saw the old hag the first time I would like you to now reverse the process. Instead of a big ugly nose there is instead a diminutive chin of an attractive young woman. Instead of a snarly looking eye you now have a somewhat delicate looking ear of a pretty young lady. Are you having difficulty seeing the other image? Keep looking until you can. Believe me, it's there. The first time I saw this picture I saw the old hag and couldn't see the young woman for a very long time. This exercise was done at Harvard Business School and was also featured in Stephen Covey's bestselling book, The 7 Habits Of Highly Effective People.

Some call this shift in perception—when you finally can see the other image—a paradigm shift. Basically, a total shift in your perception, giving you a brand new reality from the same information you had before. Through the rest of the exercises in this book we will change your paradigms—your realities—to those that advantage you instead of disadvantage you. In some cases you may feel as much of a "WOW" as you may have just experienced in the perception of the old hag/young lady paradigm you've just experienced. In other cases your paradigms may change so gradually that you may not even be aware that they are changing.

You have undoubtedly experienced paradigm shifts previously in your life. Has there ever been a case where you thought you hated a particular song, and later came to love it? Has there ever been a case where that movie you detested became one that you later enjoyed? How about a person that at one point you couldn't stand to be around, and later they came to be one of your best friends? What caused the change in your perception? Do you agree with me now that the world around you can be perceived in a multitude of ways? Our goal through the rest of this book is to help you perceive your world in a way that helps you be all you're capable of becoming. I know that is your goal as well.

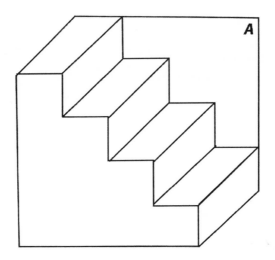

Take a look at the picture of the stairs. What do you see? If you were looking at the wall with the "A" on it as the back wall, try for a moment to look at it as the front wall. If you're like most people, you experienced a sudden paradigm shift in your perception. For me the stairs turned inside out—In fact, I had to stop looking at it as I was getting a headache. Initially, I could only see the image one way, then it kept shifting back and forth in front of my eyes.

The next image is an interesting one and also causes a "WOW" when the reality of the other paradigm kicks in. What do you see?

Most people see a vase at first, although not all do. Take a look at the picture again and see if you can see two profile images of men's faces staring eye to eye.

If you're having trouble seeing the profiles, concentrate on the white instead of the black. Now can you see the other paradigm?

Your assignment for today is a very easy one. I would like you to think of at least three situations where your perception of an event was totally different than someone you know.

1. Trump is bad.
2. Hard boil uggs are good.
3. dogs own cats

Now, I would like you to think of three perceptions that fit the other example given above, where you changed your feelings about something or someone after you gained more knowledge or for whatever reason began to look at it/them differently than you previously had.

1. Kathy like trump
2. Jen hates egg
3. I know people like cats over dogs

Have fun, and I'll see you tomorrow.

CHAPTER FOUR

UNDERSTANDING FEAR

W elcome to chapter four. You now understand that the paradigms of your perceptions about yourself and your world can be changed. The ceiling of limitations which has been programmed into your subconscious from your early years can be raised just by your making the conscious decision to do so, and taking the necessary steps to make it happen. The flea can't do this, but you can. The flea doesn't understand that its fear of hitting its head and not getting where it wants to go is what keeps it from ever jumping again. Now that you know this, you can face and conquer that fear. The first step in accomplishing this is to understand what fear really is.

RAISE THE BAR ON YOUR NEW SELF-BELIEFS!

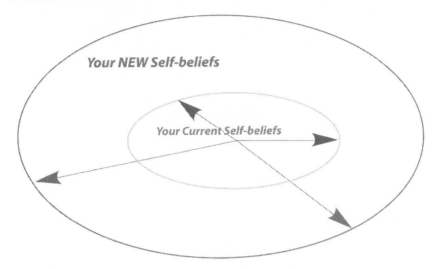

What is fear? You may remember that Franklin Roosevelt said once, "The only thing we have to fear is fear, itself." While this isn't always true, it certainly is one of the causes of all phobias. We quickly learn to fear our own fear. Fear becomes its own self-fulfilling prophecy. What happens initially is that we have an "incident" which may be caused by a real physiological response to a food—particularly a stimulant like caffeine—and the experience is so terrifying that we begin to focus on that event as something we couldn't bear to experience again. So, we alter our focus; from the world around us to more and more of the event that embarrassed us, limited us, and made us feel less than worthy.

FOCUS ON YOUR POSITIVE FUTURE!

In a very real sense we focused on the fear—we began to fear the fear. In phobias the fear of the recurring fear event can strike abject terror into our hearts and minds. Eventually the fear can become so controlling that just the thought of the event can bring all the symptoms rushing back with fury. Fear and doubt have now taken control of our lives. Remember that "We are happy and at peace with ourselves to the exact degree that we feel in control of our own lives." This will not be the last time you are reminded of that fundamental truth. Since fear has now taken away whatever control we thought we had of our own lives, the effect multiplies itself into other areas of our lives as well. If you are suffering from severe phobias you may have difficulty taking yourself back to the first event—years of negative emotions may have clouded your recollection in an effort to insulate your conscious mind from the pain. If this is true with you, you very well may be able to remember that first event vividly as you complete the step by step exercises we have constructed for you in this program. These exercises—and your understanding of the causes of your fears—are designed to remove the layers of negative emotions your mind has used to cloud your memory. You must understand that recalling the first event, understanding it, and facing it, may in and of itself allow you to erase the fear you have associated with it forever.

One definition of fear that you will want to remember is this:

F-fantasy

E-experience (becomes an *expectation*)

A-appearing

R-real

Doesn't this sound like what your fears are in most—if not all—cases of your life? Your fears aren't real at all, are they? When you were a young child you may have been afraid of monsters lurking under your bed. Now, as an adult you know that fear was silly. Maybe you were afraid of the boogieman. Are you still? Frankly, I don't even know what the boogieman is, but I doubt if you're still afraid of him. Aren't the fears you let control you now just as silly? If you think of the analysis we have just made on the causes of fear, and you now apply it to a phobia, what happens is this: The experience becomes an expectation. The first time you felt the fear it wasn't expected—that in itself made it terrifying. But, the second time—magnifying every time you mentally reviewed the first experience—it now became an expectation. You expected to be afraid, and so you were. Your personal definition of fear can now be, Fantasy *Expectation* Appearing Real.

As we progress through the chapters in this book you will learn that our expectations become our outcomes. What we expect to happen, happens—it's that simple. You will learn how to manage your expectations through a variety of methods, which have been proven to work time and time again for many thousands of people just like you. The only way these methods will not work is if you don't commit yourself to the process of making them work. Ian Fleming said, "Fear is the dividend paid to disaster before it happens." Isn't that just a different way of saying that what we expect to happen generally happens. If we look negatively at the future, one of two things will happen to us. Either our negative expectation will reap a negative outcome, or the fear and doubt created by our negative expectations will prevent us from ever even trying. Either way, we have reaped a negative result. The Bible says, "We reap what we sow." Are you sowing a negative result before you ever get there? The Bible illustration of reaping and sowing was made to appeal to people who primarily farmed for a living. They knew that if they sowed wheat seed, wheat eventually grew. Corn never grew from the planting of wheat seed. The illustration was made to show that we get out of something whatever we put into it. You know that already, don't you? But what if the farmer's expectation was that the wheat would never grow at all, or that it would be consumed and destroyed by some deadly fungus, or insects. If that were what the farmer expected to happen, what do you believe his approach to planting—sowing—the seed would be?

I recently took up motorcycle riding. Although I'm enjoying riding fully, I am not encouraging you to become a biker. I'm only writing this to make a point. In Florida we are required to take a state certified motorcycle safety course in order to legally drive a motorcycle. The course is excellent, and frankly I wouldn't have had the slightest idea of how to steer or safely handle a motorcycle without it. One of the fundamentals of controlling the bike is that wherever you are looking is where you end up going—and it happens quickly. In the driving part of the course—which normally happens in an empty parking lot—the instructors set up orange cones which the rider learns to navigate around. There are several tests you have to pass which become progressively more difficult over the two and a half day course. The instructors keep drilling it into you to turn your head fully and look in the direction you want to go in order for the bike to go there. Remember that this isn't like driving a car where the four wheels keep you upright. You really do have to develop a different—two wheeled—mentality, or you and the bike will end up on the ground or into a tree. An interesting phenomenon—and one that always happens—is that the trainees look at the orange cones in order to avoid them, and by their so doing this they always hit them. What you have to learn in order to pass the test, is not to look at the cones but to only look at where you want the bike to go. The motorcycle always goes where your eyes are focused. If you're looking at the cones—your fear in this example—then that is where you'll end up. If you're turning a corner and you're looking down at the road—your fear, again— then that's where the bike is going—down. You need to turn your head sharply and focus your eyes on your desired destination— your desired future—and that is where the bike will take you— safely and comfortably through the turn. I have to confess that the method and its results amazed me, but it works every time. At the time of writing this I've been riding now for about three months. Even though I can clearly remember my fear and uncertainty at the beginning—especially in the training course—I now do it habitually. I don't have to think about it at all. Your life works exactly the same way, and just as with the motorcycle, it works every single time. You end up going exactly where your mental focus directs you. **If you focus on your fear**—the cones—**you end up at your fear.** If you focus on the positive outcome—the safe destination in the distance where you want to go—then that is exactly where you end up. If you can just learn this simple lesson and apply it beginning today—now, and develop the habit of living this way, your life will become dramatically different from this day forward. The results will astound and amaze you.

Your assignment for today is a very important one. It is the second—but not the last—time you will be asked to visualize your future as if it had already taken place. Before you do that you will need to make a list of your fears. What doubts, anxieties, phobias, and fears are limiting you? Make a list of them right now.

1.
2.
3.
4.
5.

Starting with number one—which for most people is their biggest fear—make a list of how this fear limits you. In other words, as completely as you can, write down all the ways this fear limits you and makes you feel unhappy in any way. Let your mind flow—don't analyze what you are writing. Don't try to judge whether what you're writing is the whole truth—just write. Learn to trust yourself. Just let the words flow out of you

1.

Now do the same thing with fear number two.
2.

Fear number three:
3.

4.

5.

If you have more fears than these you may want to get your notebook or journal and continue the exercise. It's important that you be as complete as you can be.

Now, what you'll need to do is get leverage on your mind. You already know that you can pick up an entire car with the leverage provided by a good jack, or loosen a rusted bolt with a good wrench. The leverage you will now get on your mind works similarly. Your mind must understand in its totality the immense weight of the fears you have written down. What I would like you to do is to drag these fears with you—along with all the ways you are limited and hurt by them—into the future. Go one year into the future and let your mind paint the picture of your life for you. What does it look like? Who are the people that are in it? Are they happy or sad? What are the colors that you see? What are the sounds that you hear? How do you feel about your life? How do you feel about yourself?

GET LEVERAGE ON YOUR MIND
AND EXPAND YOUR WORLD..

Drag these fears five years into the future now. What is your life like? Let your mind paint as vivid a picture as it can. Ask yourself all the same questions and don't hold anything back. Letting yourself feel the disappointment is exactly what your mind needs to do.

Now go ten years into the future. What is your life like now? How do you feel about it?

Now go twenty years into the future. Ask yourself all the same questions. How do you feel?

Now comes the fun part. Allow yourself the pleasure, joy, peace, and all the other positive emotions that come with allowing yourself to imagine these fears out of your life now. Beginning today you no longer have them at all. Smile to yourself as you take yourself one year into the future. What does your life look like? Where are you? Who are the people around you? What do they look like? Are they happy? How do you feel about yourself? What are the sounds that you hear? What do you smell? What does it feel like to think about yourself with all the control you now have over your life?

Take yourself five years into the future without any of the fears, doubts, and anxieties you listed above. Ask yourself all the same questions.

Take yourself ten years into the future now—No fears at all. What do the pictures of your life look like now? What do the faces of the people around you look like? What sounds are you hearing? Where are you? What are you doing? Are you smiling and happy? How do you feel about yourself knowing that you are in control of your own life?

Take yourself twenty years into the future. Ask yourself the same questions. Allow your mind to paint the most vivid pictures of the life you want to have—a life with no fears at all. How do you feel?

Are you done with these exercises? Congratulations. Your mind has already begun to re-program itself for the new you. You're doing wonderfully. I'll see you tomorrow.

CHAPTER FIVE

WHAT IS LOVE?

W elcome to chapter five. Did you do your visualization exercises yesterday? If you did, you may already be noticing some changes in your thought processes and the way you look at yourself. If you didn't, aren't you short-changing yourself? Remember that winners take action. You're reading this book because you already are or desire to be a winner. Just understanding the logic of what you've read thus far will not be enough to change the programming of your past. If you want to be different than the flea, and raise the ceiling of your limitations, the exercises are critical for your success.

This book was written to appeal to everyone, regardless of your religious beliefs, so if you are not a religious person I hope you're not put off by this discussion. I would only ask you to keep reading with an open mind and see if you can't benefit from the thoughts expressed here. If you are religious, this chapter may open new paradigms for you, which you hadn't considered previously.

Although this is not a book about religion, I feel it is important to recognize that positive thinking can have some religious overtones. You no doubt are aware of the famous book entitled, *The Power of Positive Thinking*, by Dr. Norman Vincent Peale. You may not be aware that the original title for the book was *The Power of Faith*. Dr. Peale's publisher felt that "faith" in the title would limit the potential market for the book to a religious audience. If you think about it, though, faith and positive thinking are much the same thing. The Bible's definition of faith is "The assured expectation of things hoped for; the evident demonstration of realities though not beheld." Does this not sound like positive thinking to you? I found it interesting to learn that the Greek word used in the Bible, which is translated as faith, means "Deed of Ownership." In other words when you have faith, you are to take ownership of a future with total certainty. You no doubt will agree that if you were able to totally believe in positive outcomes for your endeavors your fears would disappear. But, you may ask, "How do I gain that total belief? How do I eliminate the doubts and the resulting fears that go along with them?" One way to accomplish that is by visualization of positive outcomes for any situation you expect to find yourself in. You have already had some practice doing this in the previous two chapters. You will want to make these positive visualizations a habit so that you don't have to make a conscious effort to do them.

If for example you are going to be giving a presentation in front of a group of people—one of the most terrifying experiences for most people—you can picture in your mind yourself giving the presentation in the most positive light. Visualize yourself standing erect and confident. Visualize the smiles on the faces of your audience as they agree with your points. If you know some of the people personally who will be in the audience—especially if they are your friends—picture yourself talking to them as they nod in appreciation. What will your friends be wearing? Picture in your mind's eye the thunderous applause as you leave the stage or podium. What will their clapping sound like? —Take the time to hear the noise. It's important that your visualizations be as real as possible. What will the colors be in the room? What will it smell like? Take the time to revel in the joy and confidence you will have leaving the stage knowing that you did a great job. What will the satisfaction of a job well done feel like? Breathe the way you will breathe when you have total confidence in yourself and your presentation. Look at yourself in the mirror as you smile confidently, fully prepared and organized to deliver material beneficial to your audience. Don't be dismayed at this point if negative thoughts keep creeping in—this is not uncommon for someone who is learning these techniques. Forgive yourself every time this happens. Remember that forgiveness is a positive emotion. Doubt is a negative emotion. You cannot harbor a negative emotion and a positive one at the same time. They are opposites of each other, like a switch either being on—positive; or off—negative. A switch is either on or off, isn't it? It can't be on and off at the same time. You can also think of 0's and 1's as in computer programming. The 1 is a completed circuit; the 0 is open. Positive thoughts lead to positive emotions, and then to positive acts. Negative thoughts lead to negative emotions, and then to negative actions. Unlike a magnet, negative and positive thoughts do not attract in our mental processes. Positives attract more positives, and negatives attract more negatives. Negative emotions are like fly paper. Negative emotions stick to negative thoughts. Every time we replace a negative thought—or a negative emotion—with a positive one, or even better, a positive action, the glue on the flypaper gets weaker. Eventually the glue will become so weak that the negative emotions—including fear—will no longer stick. Ultimately the glue won't stick at all. Believe me when I tell you that as we go through this process together it will get easier and easier. Once you re-train your mind to think positively that training will become automatic for you.

Before you read further, I would like you to write down what you believe to be the most powerful and most pure of all the positive emotions _____.

Now, what is the opposite of that? In other words, what is the purest and most destructive of all the many negative emotions _____?

All other emotions fall somewhere in between these two. If we were to draw a chart showing the spectrum of human emotions it would look something like this:

LOVE <--> **HATE**

Take a clean sheet of paper and draw a line down the middle of the sheet. On one side of the paper write down as many positive emotions as you can think of. It's important that you do this yourself before you read further. Go ahead, I'll wait.

Now on the other side of the paper I would like you to write down as many negative emotions as you can think of.

The Bible says that God is Love. This is not to say that God merely has qualities of love, but that God is Love. No matter what your religious beliefs there is an important lesson to be learned here. If God is Love, we can state this the following way:

GOD = LOVE   **LOVE = GOD**

Every time we allow ourselves the luxury of negative emotions we draw away from Love and therefore we draw away from God. Take a moment now and review the list of emotions that you have created. Wouldn't you like to feel the emotions on the positive side all the time? Sit back now and think about how your life would be different if these were the emotions you felt all day long, every day of the rest of your life. Interestingly enough, The Bible says that God's Holy Spirit provides the following fruitages: love, joy, peace, patience, kindness, goodness, faith, gentleness, and self-control. All of these fruitages are positive emotions, aren't they? You may remember the account where Jesus walked on the water of the Sea of Galilee. Peter actually walked out to meet him until he began to doubt, at which point he sank until Jesus grabbed his hand and erased his doubts. Whether we believe the Bible to be literally true or just an allegory it should make us appreciate that doubts, fears, anger, jealousy, bitterness, shortness of temper, and other negative emotions can destroy our faith and take us farther away from God—farther away from Love. Your list should look something like this:

POSITIVE EMOTIONS

Love
Joy
Peace
Patience
Kindness
Goodness
Faith
Gentleness
Self-control
Forgiveness
Selflessness (Giving to others without thought of self)
Happiness
Confidence

NEGATIVE EMOTIONS

Hate
Sadness
Anxiousness
Meanness
Anger
Ruthlessness
Doubt
Fear
Temper
Jealousy
Revenge
Covetousness
Selfishness
Depression
Sorrow

Now that you know this you might ask, "What can I do about it? How do I stop my mind from allowing the negative thoughts—emotions—from entering?" The answer is very simple. Negative thoughts and the emotions that go with them are merely habits, which we began at a very young age. When we were babies we had no fear, no doubt, none of the negative emotions which are so limiting to us now. When your parents or guardians told you, "Don't touch that, don't go there, stop that, no," and all the other negative words which were meant for your protection, your newly formed brain absorbed these thoughts totally and kept repeating them over and over in your little mind. The little voice of your thoughts is still saying, "I can't, I'm too small, I mustn't go there, I shouldn't, I'm not good enough."

Doubt ➡ Fear ➡ Anger ➡ Meanness ➡ Hate ➡ Destructive Acts

Your brain is the most powerful computer ever made. Scientists cannot begin to calculate the power of the human brain, admitting that the amount of knowledge the brain can absorb and contain is infinite. The most advanced computer that man has made to date can't even begin to compare to the power of your brain. And yet, the fundamental programming of your computer was done before you could even understand what programming is. Would you buy an expensive, powerful computer, and then hire an infant to write the operating system and software for it? And yet, that is exactly what has happened to your unconscious mind. The beautiful thing about this fact is that by merely making the decision to change the programming—rewrite the software—and taking action to do this you can change that negative programming. You can and will unlock the incredible power of your magnificent brain, not only to overcome and eliminate your fears but also to accomplish incredible things in your life.

WOULD AN INFANT PROGRAM YOUR COMPUTER?

You see, up until now you have been a car riding around with the brakes on. Depending on the level and depths of your fears you have either been a sports car with the emergency brake slightly on, or you could be trying to drive around with one foot on the gas and the other firmly applied to the brake pedal. Together, we will release the brakes. The next chapter will show you how to do this in a simple, step by step process that cannot fail. The only way it won't work for you is if you don't take the steps seriously and do them systematically. There is an old axiom that if you do something every single day for 21 days straight it becomes a habit. Will you make the commitment to yourself right now that you will take these steps? If you do, and if you follow through on your commitment to yourself, your life will change in ways you can't even imagine.

Your assignment for today is this: Every time you realize a negative thought is entering your mind, replace it with a positive one. Review the list of negative vs. positive emotions and find the positive emotion that is the opposite of each negative. Try for just today to only allow positive thoughts into your mind. Don't get mad at yourself or reprimand yourself if you realize you are thinking negatively—these emotions in themselves are negative. Forgive yourself when you realize you have slipped and think of something positive right away. Forgiveness is a positive emotion. A great method I have found is to ask myself the question, "What's something positive about this?" Let your mind give you the answer. Learn to have fun with it—don't be afraid to laugh at yourself when you mess up. Laughter is a great stress reliever, and as long as your laughter isn't at the expense of someone else it is a positive emotion. Again, for the rest of today only allow positive thoughts into your mind. A journey of a thousand miles starts with the first step. You are developing new mental habits that you will want to keep for the rest of your life. Replacing old bad habits with new good ones isn't easy, but it is well worth the effort and will pay amazing dividends for you as you go through the process of personal growth. Have fun, and I'll see you tomorrow.

Chapter Six

Like and Love Yourself

Welcome to chapter six. How did you do yesterday with focusing on positive thoughts only? I'm going to assume that you spent the entire day searching for the positives in every situation by asking yourself the question, "What positives can I find here?" Isn't life much better when we view the glass as half full instead of half empty? Wouldn't you like to think that way every day? If your answers were yes, why not try it again today. Why not make a habit of thinking that way?

Dennis Allyn

YOU MUST LOVE YOURSELF IN ORDER TO LOVE OTHERS....

We have agreed that Love is the purest of all the positive emotions. We now know that the Bible's definition of Love is God, and vice versa, and that all negative emotions that we allow to enter our minds take us further away from perfect Love—hence, further away from God. In order to continue the process of de-sticking the glue on the flypaper of your negative emotions you must love yourself. The way you feel about yourself creates the filter through which you look at everything around you. We as human beings automatically delete all information that does not match up with our beliefs. We do it without even being aware of it. Would it surprise you if I told you that if you don't like and love yourself your mind automatically interprets other people's actions towards you as negative? The filter of your beliefs won't let the positives come in. You expect them to be negative, and your mind will not allow you to be disappointed. Your beliefs become self-fulfilling prophecies.

It is impossible to love others more than you love yourself. If you want to have more friends, and better relationships, the first thing you must do is like and love yourself more than you now do. If you have children, or plan on having them you will do them a great disservice in their training and growth as human beings if you don't like and love yourself first. If you've ever flown you know that you're supposed to put the oxygen mask on yourself first, and then place it over the mouth and nose of your young child. The reason for this is that if you don't take care of yourself first in an emergency situation where oxygen is required your mind will most likely not be functioning at its optimum to effectively protect the life of your loved one. Should it surprise you to realize that your everyday life is no different? If you don't have your own mental house in order how can you expect to give your children the love they deserve and the self esteem that comes with it?

You may be thinking that only conceited or haughty people love themselves. Generally, the reverse is true. In most cases those that act this way are overcompensating for deep-seated insecurities. Those who truly love themselves are able to freely give love to others and have no need for conceit. When you truly like and love yourself completely—and you will, you will make friendships with ease. No doubt in your life you have known people who just have a way with people—who seem to attract people like a magnet. I am referring to quality people who just seem to attract other quality people who have no ulterior motives for their friendship. Perhaps you know or have known people with "magnetic personalities." We might be tempted to say, "Well, they were born with good looks, that's all it is." But, haven't you known people like this who weren't really that good-looking—they just acted like they were. Don't these individuals have a charisma about them? What is charisma? Where does it come from? Would you like to have it?

WOULD YOU LIKE A MAGNETIC PERSONALITY?

We have agreed that positive emotions attract positive emotions and that negative emotions attract negative emotions. The same is true with people. Positive people attract positive people, just as negative people attract negative people. We tend to attract into our lives the people and circumstances which harmonize with our dominant thoughts and beliefs. If you have ever wondered why you attract the people and events in your life that you do, see if this law has application in your own life. Are you positive most of the time? What types of thoughts and emotions are most prevalent in your life? How much do you truly like and love yourself? This is what we call self-esteem. If you have high self-esteem you feel good about yourself—you like yourself. It's that simple. If you truly like yourself you naturally have a high degree of self-confidence and most likely have many friends who also have a good degree of self-confidence.

Let's go through a little test and see how much you like yourself. Ask yourself the following questions, and be totally honest with yourself. If you want to overcome your negative, limiting thoughts and beliefs—and I doubt you'd be reading this book if you didn't—you must be honest with your own self-appraisal. The first step of change is identifying what it is that needs changing. Remember again that this is your book. It is a permanent record for you to look back on in the months, and years to come to verify the progress you have made in becoming the person you desire to be. Write your answers in the space provided. If the category doesn't apply to you, simply leave it blank. How much do I like myself as a:

Parent:

Daughter or son:

Student:

Friend:

Employee:

Supervisor:

Spiritual person:

Brother or sister:

How much do I like myself in the following?

My weight:

My appearance:

My energy level:

My health:

What have I learned from the above?

What changes do I need to make to like myself more in the areas I am unhappy with?

What did you learn about your level of self-like and self-love? If you don't like some of your answers, don't despair. Remember that this thirty-day program is a process of change. All you have done here is to identify what needs to be changed. Most people never take the trouble to take even this first step. You have already made major progress just by the realization that you are not where you want to be in these areas. You have just taken a major step in a process known as goal setting. Later on you will learn how to go about achieving these goals, but the first step is identifying what they are.

For example, in your answers to the questions, how much did you like yourself in the area of your weight? If you answered not very much, what would a goal be? —In other words, what would make you like yourself in this area?

How about the question of "as a friend?" How much do you like yourself in this area? If you are not as good a friend as you could be, why not? What would you like to change? Don't worry about the "how will I do this" part right now. We'll get to that later.

Your assignment for this chapter is this: Take each of the areas we have just identified and write specific goals for what you would like to be in order to really like yourself in those categories. If there are areas that come to your mind that aren't listed, great—write them down. Remember that the more you like yourself, the better your self esteem, and the easier it will be for you to become the person you desire to be in every area of your life. You'll have better relationships with your family, better friendships, more success in your career, and much better peace of mind and happiness. Have fun, and I'll see you tomorrow.

CHAPTER SEVEN

FORGIVE YOURSELF

Welcome to chapter seven. Did you finish yesterday's exercise? If you did, congratulations. If not, please take the time right now to identify what areas of your life you see some weaknesses in. Remember that your degree of self-like and self-love affects every single area of your life. A positive self-esteem is critical for you in your journey to become the person you desire to be, and having the life you want for yourself. As we've said, it also affects everyone around you, particularly those you care about. If you won't do it for yourself, doesn't it make sense to do it for them?

WRITE YOURSELF A LETTER..

If you bought this book you most likely are one of two types of people. You either are a fairly successful, happy, individual who wants to unlock some of your unused potential, or you may feel controlled by fear. If you are of the second type, you may be a very unhappy person. You may have severe phobias, you may be chronically depressed, or you may have even considered taking your own life. **The first thing you must do in either case is to forgive yourself for feeling the way you do—forgive yourself totally.** Remember this; everyone has fears, some are worse than others, but everyone has them. You are not alone. I wrote this book because I have felt controlled by my own fears for much of my life. Even though I conveyed an image of self-confidence to the outside world I was a scared little boy inside my own mind. Because of this I placed myself on a personal mission—to find the causes of fear and to eliminate them from my life. The past is history, the future a mystery; today is a gift, that's why we call it the present. We must learn to forget the past and plan positive outcomes for the future while thoroughly enjoying the present—a gift that comes each and every day.

Actually, the process is very simple—that's not to say that it is easy, but it is simple. Anyone—including you—can do it if you really have the desire to do so. The fact that you have made the investment in this book proves that you have the desire—now you simply have to follow the steps I will outline for you. Believe me when I tell you that if you do, your fears can be overcome and even eliminated forever. The first thing you must do—do it now before you read any further— is forgive yourself. You must forgive yourself totally and completely. The best way to do this—as silly as it may sound at first—is to write a letter to yourself. Write it as completely as you can and in as much detail as you can outlining what you are holding against yourself. You may be wondering what purpose writing a letter to yourself could possibly serve. I can answer this by saying that when you write something down it has permanence that thinking to yourself could never have.

WOULD YOU HONOR A CONTRACT MADE ONLY IN THOUGHT? OR, WOULD YOU DEMAND IT IN WRITING?

Almost all of the communication we do with ourselves is through our thought processes—that little voice in our heads. Sometimes we are aware of the voice, but most of the time we are not. Later on we'll discuss how to hear what the voice is saying to you—you may be surprised. If you have been controlled by your own fears up until now I can guarantee you that most of what the voice says is negative, maybe frighteningly so. These negative messages have been programmed in your mind from your earliest days. In order to eliminate fear from your life these negative messages must be replaced with positive ones. We will show you how to do this—don't be concerned with that now. When something is really important, such as the sale of a piece of property, we write it down. When you do a Will, you write it down, even having it officially notarized and witnessed because of its importance. When we really want to make an impression on someone we love we send him or her a written message. When you are finished writing down all the things you are holding against yourself, tell yourself that it's okay—it's in the past and you cannot change a thing about the past no matter how much you would like to. It does you no good whatsoever to harbor animosity or ill will towards yourself for any past behaviors, be they real or imagined. If you have hurt others—as we all have—forgive yourself. If you have made mistakes—as we all have, no matter how major they may have been—forgive yourself completely. If you have failed to accomplish your goals, forgive yourself. If you haven't lived up to the expectations of others, forgive yourself.

Now, before you turn the page, sit yourself down and write the letter to yourself. This is a totally private process for you. Only you need know what you write, but you must tell yourself that you forgive yourself completely and unequivocally. Hold nothing back. Let the emotional release of this forgiveness flow from you. Don't be surprised if you experience a catharsis you have never felt before— this is not unusual. Now, write the letter and then come back to the book. Go ahead, I'll wait.

Now that you have written the letter I would like you to consider doing something really silly. Why not put the letter in an envelope, address it to yourself, put a stamp on it—correct postage of course— and drop it in the mailbox. If there is something in the letter that you desire to remain private and you're afraid someone else will open it then by all means don't do this part. If that is the case you can even burn the letter to ashes, but in burning it, burn your anger and guilt as well. Remember that the past is gone—it cannot be changed. If you can, though, mail the letter to yourself. When you receive it in a few days it will re-affirm your forgiveness.

You have now taken a very important first step—forgiving yourself completely. And you haven't done it with just a voice in your head or even by looking in the mirror and saying out loud, "I forgive myself," (which by the way looks really silly if anyone else is around). No, you have actually taken the time to write yourself a letter and make a permanent hard copy of your forgiveness. In a sense you have made a contract with yourself. I would be very surprised if you have ever done this before—don't underestimate its power. You have also done something else; you have taken positive **action** to overcome your fears. No matter what anyone else may have led you to believe thus far, you are the only one that can overcome and eliminate the fears that have limited you up until now—no one else can do it for you.

What does forgiving myself have to do with fear, you may ask? Simple. Fear is a negative emotion, one of the most damaging anyone can have. Forgiveness is a positive emotion—again, one of the most powerful anyone can have. As we have discussed, it is impossible to hold a negative emotion and a positive emotion at the same time. By the time our journey—yours and mine—is complete, you will eliminate negative emotions from your thought processes. Your mind will not accept a vacuum. The negative thoughts and emotions must be replaced with positive ones. This job must be done one step at a time. Believe me, you have taken an important first step to eliminating fear from your life.

If you've written the letter to yourself your assignment for today is finished. Congratulate yourself. Look in the mirror and smile at yourself—you've done well. If you haven't as yet written it, please don't put it off—do it now. I'll see you tomorrow.

Chapter Eight

Forgive Others Freely

Welcome to chapter number eight. Did you write yourself the letter yesterday? If not, why not? If you just put it off, can you take the time to write it now?

Can You Forgive?

It's possible that you cannot bring yourself to write the letter at all. Do you feel that your past mistakes have been so severe that you can't bring yourself to forgive yourself? We have stated in these pages that the past is the past—you can't change it. This is a fact that is indisputable. Even though the past is over you may realize that the harms caused by you in the past have consequences for others in their lives today, and in their futures that don't go away by you just forgiving yourself. Is there anything you can do to make it right? Ask yourself the question, "What can I do to make amends for those I have harmed?" This may be difficult to answer. Since I don't know you personally, I do not know if your past wrongs merely hurt someone's feelings, or if you have done grievous harm. It is possible that you have done great harm to no one, or that you have done great damage to many. Maybe those you have harmed are not even alive anymore. Maybe you have no idea where they are. I leave it to you to decide how hard you should try to find them or their loved ones. If you're serious about starting a new life, can you make amends to their family somehow? If that is impossible, what can you do to help others that might in some way make amends—at least in your mind—for your past errors? I leave the rest to you. I wish you well.

Whatever you have decided you must understand that you can't succeed in the journey we have started together until you have forgiven yourself for your past. It is possible that the information in the rest of this chapter may help you forgive yourself as well as others.

Is there anyone in your life—present or past—who you hold anger, resentment, animosity, or hate for? Has there been anyone in your life who you feel has really done you wrong? It could be your parents, your siblings, a friend or friends. It could be a teacher you once had, or a former lover. It could be your mate, or ex-mate. It could even be a faceless stranger; someone who you never met who harmed you in some way. Search your memory if you must—this is important.

Remember our discussion of positive and negative emotions. If you are harboring these negative feelings you must understand that they are greatly affecting your growth as a human being and are harming you again every time you remember them. Even if you are not consciously thinking of these memories they are there, in your sub-conscious mind, holding you back. Every negative thought, emotion, or memory that you allow to dwell within your mind is pushing away the positive emotions that will release your personal power, erase your fears and doubts, and allow you to be the complete, happy, and successful person you desire and deserve to be. Ask yourself this very important question: "Who is being harmed by these feelings, them or me?" If someone sticks you with a pin and causes you tremendous pain, who is hurt by you remembering that event over and over again—you or them? Remember that every time you replace a negative thought with a positive one, or a negative emotion with a positive one, you release more of the brakes that are holding you back from reaching your full potential.

Recent psychological studies prove that those who forgive easily enjoy better mental and physical health than those who harbor feelings of anger, hostility, and revenge. Psychologist Michael McCullough, of the National Institute for Healthcare Research says, "Unless they're repeatedly excusing someone who's abusive, forgiveness seems to be a positive act for the one doing it." Everett Worthington of Virginia Commonwealth University, in his studies of 214 adults, concluded that refusal to forgive is most common among people with high anger and fear levels. Humility, however, encourages people to let go of slights or betrayals. Charlotte vanOyen of Hope College discovered that just forming images in the mind of a past betrayal or hurtful event raised heart rate and blood pressure and caused significant worsening of mood. On the contrary, thinking of forgiveness reversed these patterns. June Tangney, of George Mason University, in her studies of 285 adults, found that those with highest self-esteem readily forgave themselves but had some difficulty forgiving others. She found that depressed, angry people had the most trouble forgiving. Dwelling on the hurt caused significant worsening of mood.

WHY KEEP RE-LIVING IT?

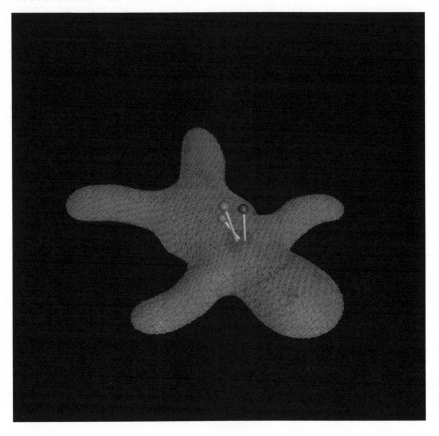

I know that what I'm asking you to do may be difficult. You may believe that the person deserves your hate and anything bad that can happen to them. I am not saying here that they don't. The point is this; you are the one being damaged by your hate, not them. As you think right now about whatever actions or treatment this person inflicted upon you does it affect them at all? Most likely not. I am not suggesting here that it is necessary or even beneficial for you to keep this person/persons in your life. In fact, it may be necessary for you to end all association with them. This is up to you totally. All I am saying is that you must forgive them.

For many people it is their parents for whom they harbor the most animosity. If this is the case with you, maybe you feel that your parents didn't give you the love or support you deserved and needed. Maybe Mom/Dad treated your brother or sister better than they treated you. Maybe they were physically, emotionally, or even sexually abusive. These behaviors no doubt have left deep scars in your sub-conscious mind. No one can blame you for harboring the feelings that you have, but you must re-frame your memories—look at them in a new light, and create new associations to their actions. Our brains have made associations to every event in our lives. This has happened since the day we were born and continues to happen until the day we die. Every event is either associated with pain or pleasure. Our deepest set associations were made when we were very young, but new ones are being made all the time. You are the one who can consciously re-program your mind to associate these past experiences in any way you choose. Doesn't it make sense to make associations that empower you and help you grow as opposed to those that limit you? The easiest way to look at re-framing any negative experience is to ask yourself the question, "What can I learn from this that will make me a better person and benefit those around me?" Your magnificent computer-like brain will search and search until it comes up with positive answers to any positively asked question. If you ask the question with the expectation of an answer your mind will give you one—and, it will be a good one. You now have re-associated a negative (pain causing) experience with a positive outcome. Any experience in your life can be learned from in a positive way.

Recently I saw a documentary about the Vietnam War where American Vietnamese War Veterans who experienced terrible events in active duty in Vietnam were taken back to the same fields, buildings, towns, and cities where the original horrors occurred. Many of these men had experienced or continued to experience PTSD (posttraumatic stress syndrome) from these memories. Some still harbored hatreds for the VC (Viet Cong) who killed or maimed their buddies and themselves in war. They had the opportunity to meet, talk, and even eat and drink with men who were formerly soldiers, and officers in the North Vietnamese army. It was exciting to see them re-frame (make new associations in their minds) these events by looking at the war in a different way than they had previously. Several of these men began to cry as memories long since repressed resurfaced in their minds with full force. But, now they could see that from the perspective of the former enemy, he had been fighting for his country's freedom; the United States was the invader. To them it was a civil war, much the same as the United States looks at its own Civil War. These men—formerly enemies—laughed and cried together as they forgave one another for the pain and suffering each caused the other. The evil former enemy now was looked at in a different light. He was now just a man. A man with fears, doubts of his own, children, a wife, a job, likes and dislikes; just a man.

They shared with each other—Vietnamese and Americans— stories of the friends, family, and relatives they had lost in the war. Of course it was the Vietnamese who lost their families, as it was their homeland that endured the bombing, Agent Orange, and other weapons of destruction used by the Americans in the war. And yet, they were willing to forgive. Every American interviewed afterwards said that a terrible weight finally lifted from them. They now felt free in a way they hadn't felt since the war. What can you and I learn from this? By looking at terrible past experiences from a different perspective they were able to re-frame the events in their minds. They were also able to forgive, and this forgiveness allowed all the fears, which had re-played like scenes from a movie over and over in their minds for many years, to finally disappear. Can you benefit from this experience in your own life? Granted, some might say that they were allowed to forgive and look at these memories differently because of all the years—over 30—which had passed since the horror. But, I say, "Why wait thirty years?" There are many Vietnam War Vets in the United States who still experience the traumatic effects of the war. Time in and of itself has not erased the memories and replaced the negative associations with positive outcomes. The individual himself/herself must do that. You don't have to wait. All the waiting accomplishes is robbing you of much of the joy your life should have now. The forgiveness and the change of outlook of the event can happen right now, not some time in the distant future. It is all up to you. Remember, you control what goes into your mind, and how you perceive every event in your life. You have the power to look at any event in a positive way or a negative one. By asking yourself the right questions you can release the incredible power of your mind to give you the answers that empower you.

Today's assignment may be the most difficult emotionally for you out of this entire thirty-day program, but it is one I believe you will greatly benefit from. If you take the easy way out and don't do it you will not fully experience the benefits of the positive emotions just waiting to empower you and allow you to become all you are capable of.

Who are the individuals in my life who have hurt me, physically or emotionally abused me and caused me pain and sadness?

Write the individual/individuals a letter in as much detail as you can. What pain has he/she caused you and when? What did he/she do? Why? What experiences in the person's life at that time may have caused them to act the way they did? Remember that they no doubt had their own demons, which they had not learned to control and re-program as you now have. Feel sorry for them. Forgive them completely. Your growth and development cannot fully blossom until you do. If this person/persons is still alive and you feel that they would benefit from receiving this letter, then go ahead and mail it to them, first making a copy for yourself. The healing when they receive the letter may additionally reward you. If you feel it unnecessary or possibly harmful to your growth to send the letter, then don't. However, you must know in your heart that your forgiveness is complete and total. You must absolutely and unequivocally forgive for the negative emotions connected with the event to disappear. Now ask yourself this question, and expect with complete confidence that your wonderful mind will provide you just the perfect answer: "How can I use this experience to grow in a positive way for the benefit of myself and others around me?" Congratulations! You have made another major step toward your full development as a human being. Be proud of yourself, you've done well. I'll see you tomorrow.

CHAPTER NINE

THE POWER OF THE SUBCONSCIOUS MIND

Welcome to chapter nine. Many scientists believe that every experience, every sensory input, be it through your eyes, ears, nose, taste, or touch, every event of your life—positive and negative—is recorded in your subconscious mind. We can think of it as a giant movie library or hard-drive of our lives. Except that this movie library doesn't just have moving pictures and sound, but also the tastes, smells, and our feelings, which we experienced during these events, permanently recorded. We've already agreed that your computer-like brain is the most marvelous creation—or accident of nature—that exists in mankind's experience. Scientists don't totally understand how it works, although they know that electro-chemical reactions travel across the neurons in our brains and somehow—we don't know how—are recorded as memories.

A LIBRARY OF YOUR LIFE?

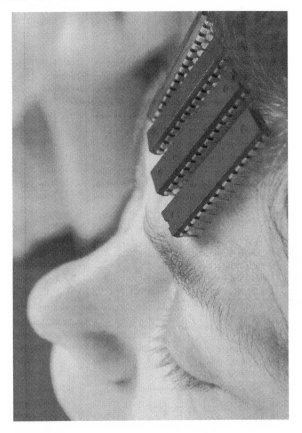

We know that there is no known limit to how much knowledge (bits of data, if we want to compare this to digital references) that the brain can store. I've read estimates—which vary widely—that say even Albert Einstein may have used only 1% or less of his brain capacity. It is widely believed that he may have been the smartest human who ever lived. If that is true, how much of your brain is just sitting there untapped?

You may have difficulty believing all of this if you sometimes forget what you had for dinner last night, or you can't remember your anniversary or when your children were born, and yet we know it is true. How do we know? There have been many scientific experiments done to prove this, which we can talk about, but you have experienced things in your own life that will allow you to prove it to yourself. I'll give you an example from my own life, which happened just recently. A couple of weeks ago I had a dream about a high school friend of mine who I literally hadn't thought about in over thirty years. His face and voice and actions were so vivid it was if it was still 1969. When I woke up I couldn't understand why my brain conjured up a person from my past. When I told my son about it he suggested that I look his picture up in my high school yearbook. The yearbook helped everything become clear. I found his picture in the seniors section where he had written a message saying, "Always remember our time together in Brigadoon, signed Bill." After thinking about it the answer came clear. What had happened was, a few days earlier my daughter had bought me the CD of the Broadway version of the musical Brigadoon. You may remember the story of a small village in Scotland that appears only once every 100 years, for only one day. Gene Kelly starred in the film version. Bill and I had been in the play together over 30 years earlier. My conscious mind had not only forgotten this experience completely, but had forgotten that Bill ever existed in my life. And yet, somehow my subconscious mind connected the music to a memory and decided to put this old friend—just as he looked over 30 years ago—in my dream. I couldn't begin to tell you why my mind did this, or if there was any particular significance to it, but the point is clear. Your mind has all the records of your life just stored away for your use if only you have the codes to access it. All you need to do is understand how your mind functions and you can use this incredible database of knowledge to your benefit at any time.

Another proof of this is the testing that scientists have done by applying electric stimulus to different areas of people's brains. Experiences long since forgotten by the conscious mind are resurrected in exact detail. Hypnosis has sometimes helped people to remember details of an event long since forgotten by the conscious mind. You may know people who have Alzheimer's, or are suffering from senility in one form or another, who can remember vividly experiences and people from their youth, but they can't remember yesterday. Have you ever had this experience? You can't remember someone's name, or possibly the name of a song you used to love. It's driving you crazy, but no matter how hard you try you can't come up with the answer. Later on that day or maybe the next day when you're not thinking about it at all, suddenly the correct answer pops into your head like magic. If you're like me, you awaken in the middle of the night with a start, and there it is. Your conscious mind didn't have the information, but your subconscious did. Think of the possibilities: Every movie and TV show you've ever watched, every book you've ever read, every joke and fable you've ever heard, all of your life's training and knowledge is at your disposal if you simply learn how to tap into it.

Believe it or not, the progress you've made thus far in reading this book and practicing the exercises we have outlined for your benefit is already leading you to the secrets of your subconscious. The reason many of these memories are difficult for you to tap is that they are buried under layers and layers of negative thoughts and emotions, which blocks their easy access by your conscious mind. By developing the habits you've already learned and replacing your negative thoughts and emotions with positive ones, the hard-drive of your subconscious mind will become easier and easier for you to access at will. Much of the ability to do this comes from your belief in yourself, and the belief that it can be done—faith. What we've already learned to call positive expectations. You know that for your faith—belief in positive outcomes—to grow, you must eliminate negative emotions from your life. By overcoming and eliminating your doubts, fears, anxieties, and all the other negative emotions that stick to them, you unlock your true potential. As you do this, your confidence continues to grow exponentially; your belief in yourself allows you to take risks that you previously wouldn't have considered. You begin your day expecting things to go well, and they do. By combining this new found confidence with the other habits you've learned—of asking yourself the right questions each day—you will begin to know that your mind will always provide the right answer if the question is asked the right way with the belief that the answer will come. The results will astound and excite you.

WHAT'S YOUR LITTLE VOICE TELLING YOU?

Your subconscious also controls the little voice that talks to you all day long. It's important for your continued development that you know what the voice is saying to you. If you doubt that there is a little voice in your head talking to you, let me ask you this question: You're hearing voices right now aren't you? As you read my words do you not hear a little voice in your head saying the words? Whose voice is it? Does it sound like your own voice? To some of us it does, and to others it doesn't. What about when you're not reading, do you hear voices then? What are your thoughts? Aren't they little voices in your own head? For most of us our thoughts happen without us even realizing that there really is a little voice talking to us—sometimes it may be more than one. For instance, I can think about a conversation I've been involved in with several people in the past and I can actually hear several different voices carrying on a conversation in my own mind. If I try I can imagine a conversation with one or more people that hasn't even happened and I can actually hear their voices in my mind. Am I crazy? Well, maybe, but I don't think so. In fact, I know that you can and most likely do the same thing.

In order for you take the next important step to overcoming and eliminating your personal fears and replacing the negative programming in your powerful computer-like brain you need to be aware of the voice/voices that are talking to you all the time. For simplicity I will refer to it as the voice (singular) from now on, but remember, all of us can actually hear more than one. The voice is controlled for the most part by your subconscious and it speaks to you based on the programming, which you and your environment put into it a long time ago. If you have severe phobias I guarantee that the voice is telling you extremely negative, harmful things on a regular basis. It may be telling you that you are worthless, that you can't do anything right, that you are unattractive, unintelligent, and that if you even try to go out of the house something terrible is likely to happen. It may even be telling you that the only way you will ever get any peace is to kill yourself. In fact, the voice may have even suggested ways for you to take your own life. Think with me for a moment what effect we would have on a child that from the time they were extremely young we told him or her constantly that they were ugly, stupid, worthless, and would never achieve anything worthwhile. Not only that, but as they were going out the door to school the very first day we told them that something terrible was most likely to happen to them that day, that their teachers wouldn't like them, and their fellow students would most likely treat them cruelly. What would their expectations be as they got on the bus? When this child really does try its hardest we spank it and tell it how disappointed we are and how ashamed that it was only able to do that much. What kind of self-esteem would you expect this child to have as they grew up?

Many of us say things to ourselves every day, all day long that we wouldn't dream of saying to those we care about. Remember that to reach our maximum potential and to be able to give love freely we must like and love ourselves. Using the example in the paragraph above, how do you expect to like and love yourself if you constantly say things to yourself you would never say to a loved one? If the child's life we described above resembles yours, I am sorry. However, you must realize that yesterday does not have to affect today, or tomorrow, for that matter. Were you scared of the dark when you were little? My son is thirteen years old and many times even now he sleeps with the light on in his room. This isn't at all uncommon for a child. What about so-called haunted houses that you may have gone through as a child at Halloween. Were they terrifying to you?

Chances are, for most of us, the things that terrified us as children are not that scary anymore. I would imagine that when my son grows up he won't need to sleep with the light on. In fact, many times he forgets to turn it on now. Sometimes, he remembers his fear of the dark and feels he needs that security. Did you have a woobie (security blanket) when you were a little child? My daughter did. In fact, she couldn't go to bed without her woobie. At twenty years of age she still has it. It's so old and ragged now and has been washed—thank goodness—so many times that it bears scant resemblance to the nice yellow blanket it once was. As I write this my daughter is on her honeymoon and guess what? She forgot to take her woobie! What's the point? That as we grow up our perspective of the world around us changes. We look at the world with an adult outlook instead of the insecure outlook of a little child in a big scary world. What may not have changed, however, as you grew, is the basic programming that your little child-like mind absorbed earlier in your life. The exciting part of all this is that you have the power to change that programming now.

GIVE YOURSELF THE RIGHT MESSAGES

Before we give you the methods to change the programming it is important for you to hear the voice and be aware of what it is telling you. What I would like you to do is to go to a place where you can have total quiet for at least a half an hour or more. Right now, before you read any further I'd like you to get in a quiet place, all by yourself, with no possibility of distractions—turn off your cell phone, radio, TV, beeper, telephone ringer, etc. Places where I've had success are in my parked car, in my bedroom, in the bathtub, in my office, even in the closet if that's what it took to get away—this last one turned out interesting when my wife discovered me in there. Another place that works wonderfully is the park if you can find a nice quiet place where you're by yourself. If this is impossible for you right now then I challenge you to make an appointment with yourself to do this exercise at your earliest opportunity—it's essential to your growth. In the total silence where you eventually become aware of your own breathing and even possibly the beating of your heart you will eventually be able to hear the little voice. As you visualize situations that normally cause you stress and anxiety, what is the voice saying? Chances are it is giving you negative messages of varying degrees. It may be saying, "I can't," or "Why bother? I'm not good enough," or "He/she won't like me anyway." Or, it may be asking "what if" questions. "What if I freeze up?" or "What if someone attacks me?" or "What if he/she doesn't like me?" What's crucial for you to realize is this: You have the absolute power as an adult to re-write the software of your unconscious mind so that the little voice says things like, "Go ahead, try it, you're a winner," or "You can do anything you set your mind to do, you always win." Pinocchio had Jimini Cricket as his conscience, giving him advice all day long and trying to keep him out of trouble. If it helps you to make believe that Jimini is on your shoulder giving you the positive messages you need to motivate you, go ahead. Eventually your mind will be programmed through these exercises to say the right things instead of the negative self-talk you may be receiving now. Now, let's go back to our example of the little child that we constantly fed negative thoughts, and change the game. Now we have a little child that is reinforced in a positive way at every stage of their growth and development. They are constantly told how pretty or handsome they are, how smart they are, how everyone will like them, how their teachers want them to do well and will help them in any way that they can. This child is constantly hugged and congratulated for doing his/her best. Do you think this child will view its world differently than the first child? You better believe they will.

Your assignment for today is to go to your place of solitude and totally relax. If you have no breathing difficulties, which would prevent you from doing so, concentrate on breathing from the diaphragm. Inhale deeply through your nose, hold the breath for a second or two and slowly exhale through your mouth. Do this ten times in a row while clearing your mind of conscious thoughts. For at least thirty minutes try not to think about anything. Starting with the tips of your toes, imagine that a feeling of total calm is slowly creeping up your body. Allow your legs, then your torso to completely relax. Let the same feeling spread from the tips of your fingers up your arms to your chest. Allow the complete relaxation to reach your face. Feel your facial muscles completely relax. Some find it useful to count backwards from 100 slowly. The key here is to relax enough so that there is nothing occupying your concentration at the conscious level. After thirty minutes or so you should be able to hear the little voice of your thoughts. Once you identify it, listen to what it says. As you continue your progress you will want to remain aware of the voice's communication with you. Have fun. I'll see you tomorrow.

Chapter Ten

Happy thoughts

Welcome to chapter ten. Were you able to hear the "little voice" of your thoughts yesterday when you allowed yourself to totally relax? You will want to keep yourself aware of what your thoughts are telling you so that the message is what you desire it to be. Remember that you have the ability now as an adult to have the voice encourage you constantly, feeding you a regular diet of up-building positive information instead of the destructive negativism that may have been programmed before.

You no doubt are familiar with the story of Peter Pan. Do you remember what Peter had to do when he wanted to fly? That's right, he had to think happy thoughts. Do you remember that Wendy and the others also had to think happy thoughts? You are exactly the same way. If you truly want to release your inner power and achieve all the things in your life you have dreamed of you must learn to think happy thoughts. This sounds pretty obvious, doesn't it? Let me ask you then, if it's so obvious then why aren't you doing it? Sure, you no doubt are happy once in awhile. Maybe you're even fairly happy a good portion of the time. But, wouldn't you like to feel happy and joyful all the time? Maybe you won't fly like Peter and Wendy, or on second thought, maybe you will. Impossible, you say. Let's try something right now and see if you can think happy thoughts whenever you want to. If you can then I'd like to ask you, "Why can't you be happy and joyful all the time?" Even if you miss the mark once in awhile you can turn it into a positive experience by simply forgiving yourself—a positive emotion—and learning from it. Developing these mental habits is essential to releasing your brakes, eliminating your fears, and achieving your true potential as a human being.

Take yourself to your place of solitude where there are no disturbances. Ask yourself this question, "Was there ever a time and a place where I felt happy and at peace?" When was it? Where was it? Take yourself there now. If nothing comes to your mind then how about this question, "Where do I think I might be happy?" Close your eyes and completely relax—the harder it is for you to completely relax the more important it is for you to do it. Take a deep breath, hold it for a few seconds and then slowly exhale. Do this ten times in a row with your eyes closed. Let yourself go to that place now. What does it look like? Are there trees? What color are the leaves? Is there a breeze? What does it feel like against your skin? Does the breeze make a sound as it rushes past the leaves? What does it sound like? Are there flowers? What are their colors? What do they smell like? Are you near the ocean? What does the salt mist smell like? Does it tickle your nose? What does it feel like against your face? What do the waves sound like as they roll into the shore? Feel the sensations in your body, hear the sounds, see the sights, smell the smells. What is your breathing like in this special place? Let yourself be aware of your breathing. Do you feel a smile coming to your lips? You see, you can think of happy thoughts whenever you want to. Whenever you start to feel anxious, feel doubts, panic or fears, you can take yourself to this special place. The more you practice this the easier it will be to take yourself there at any time. This is one type of visualization technique.

TAKE YOURSELF TO YOUR SPECIAL PLACE

Another is when you know you will have to do something that would normally cause you fear or anxiety and you visualize doing it with positive outcomes. Once you have mastered taking yourself to your special—happy—place, you can take yourself there anytime and while still basking in that special glow you feel, go to the other visualization. If your fears are relatively minor you can tie the second type of visualization into the first fairly rapidly. If you are overcoming serious phobias give yourself some time. It's important that you have mastered going to your special place—your happy thoughts—before you visualize positive outcomes for your phobia event. Don't try to rush yourself—you'll know when the time is right. When you're ready you can visualize yourself in any future activity that would normally cause you fear while you visualize positive experiences during that event. If it's a talk in front of a group of people, a job interview, meetings with your boss, going into an elevator, an airplane, or just going outside your home, visualize a positive experience. Let the good feelings you feel in your special place transfer to the other experience. Keep the smile on your face as you achieve success in your new endeavor. While you're still in your restful state visualize yourself walking away from that experience knowing in your heart that you did exceptionally well. Allow yourself to feel the glowing satisfaction of a job well done. Congratulate yourself. Look in the mirror and smile at yourself. Tell yourself out-loud—hopefully you're alone or you might get some strange looks— "You did well, you're **good**!"

If you had negative thoughts or feelings enter your mind when you went to your happy place, that's okay—you'll get better at it every time you do it. Next time if negative thoughts come into your mind just say softly, "I'm not going to think about that now," and continue on with your visualization. If you still felt some anxiety when you visualized an activity that would normally cause you anxiety, forgive yourself—positive emotion. You'll do better next time. Remember that you are changing many years of bad mental habits. And, there's something else you need to know; this isn't like exercising your muscles where the adage is, "No pain, no gain." To increase muscle strength we need to take the muscles to the point of fatigue. This process is the exact opposite of that. Mental exercises should be easy and relaxed. The harder you push your mind the less successful you will be at accomplishing your goal. If you put stress on yourself, that causes anxiety—a negative emotion. Remember that we only want positives in our minds, and in our lives.

Your exercise for today is to take yourself to your place of solitude and go through the process described above. If you've done it already, congratulations. If not, please do it now. Have fun and I'll see you tomorrow.

Chapter Eleven

Heroes and Self-Beliefs

W elcome to chapter eleven. Did you have fun thinking happy thoughts? It's exciting to know that you can take yourself to your special place any time you want, isn't it? Now that you know how, wouldn't you like to take yourself there often?

Change your filter...

We've agreed that your beliefs about yourself are the filter through which your mind accepts or rejects all information coming into it. What does a filter do? That's right, a filter allows certain things to pass through and does not allow others. Have you ever panned for gold? If you haven't done this yourself, you probably know someone who has, or at least you understand the process. You have a strainer, which allows water, sand, and other unwanted elements to pass through, but does not allow the gold nuggets to pass through. You kneel in a stream where gold has been found before—you hope—and you hold the special pan in the path of the stream. Eventually, if you are fortunate enough, some of the gold nuggets get caught in the strainer.

Your mind does the same thing all the time without your conscious awareness of it. Based on the profile of yourself you have stored away, all the data coming at you 24 hours a day—even your dreams—gets filtered. Only the information that is consistent with your beliefs about yourself is allowed in. That which isn't consistent gets filtered out. This process is called editing. Just as an editor at a magazine, newspaper, or some other publishing house deletes information from the copy that he/she doesn't want in the final piece, the editor of your beliefs does the same thing. This mental editing is continual. What are your beliefs about yourself? Remember that you are not what you believe you are; but, whatever you believe, you are. To become the person you want to be you need to identify the belief system you currently have and harmonize it with your goals. If the two don't match, your goals will never be realized fully and you will feel constant anxiety without even knowing why. If you begin to achieve your goals but your belief system doesn't support your new life, your subconscious mind will begin to sabotage you to make the reality of your life consistent with your internal image of yourself.

One example of the filter allowing in the information consistent with our beliefs is one every Mother, and many Fathers can easily relate to. If you've ever had your child—particularly a teenager—demand that you help them find something in the cupboard or the refrigerator you know what I mean. You finally get up and go look—and there it is, right in front of them. How could they have not seen it? You ask yourself. Simple: They either went to the cupboard believing they wouldn't find it, or they didn't care enough to allow their mind to see it. The shows that our desires and determination to achieve the goals we set out for ourselves also greatly affects how we perceive the world around us. By focusing our mental energies on the areas that are consistent with our goals—as well as our beliefs—our mind allows the right information to enter.

I live in Florida, the Sunshine State. Most of the time we have to wear sunglasses, not just to keep from squinting, but to protect our eyes from the sun's intensity. Most sunglasses now have UV type lenses, which filter out the harmful ultraviolet rays of the sun. This filter allows the information we want to enter into our eyes and deletes the glare and harmful UV rays. Your beliefs are your filter for all the information that enters your eyes, ears, sense of smell, sense of touch, and taste. All information is selectively deleted—filtered—based on your beliefs. If you want to look at the world in a positive light you simply need to change the filter. Believe me, I have done this with myself, as have thousands of others. You can do it, too.

No doubt there are people you know personally who you greatly admire. People you would love to be like. In order to do this exercise you need to know them well enough to be able to make a pretty good guess about their beliefs about themselves. Out of everyone you know, whom do you have the greatest admiration and respect for? Who would you pick for number two on your list? Go ahead and finish in order of those people who you personally know who you admire and respect the most.

1.
2.
3.
4.
5.

Look at the first name on your list. Would you say he/she has a positive self-image? Chances are your answer is yes. Is this person confident in their abilities? Is he/she someone who takes action or who waits for things to happen to them? Are they committed to something in a positive way? Would you say they like themselves?

Have they taken the steps to control their own life or does life generally control them? Do fears, doubts, and anxiety control them, or do they have a positive outlook about themselves and those around them? Do they generally procrastinate, or are they someone who "does it now?" On a scale of 1-10 with 10 being the highest, what is this person's energy level compared to others of their age? Is this number one person on your list passionate about life or lackadaisical and uninterested? Do they care about others? Do they give of themselves to others? Now go ahead and ask the same questions about each of the others on your list. I don't know you personally, but my bet would be that most of the answers for these people you admire and respect the most out of everyone you know are positive. Chances are you believe that they like themselves, are confident in their abilities, are people of action, have generally positive outlooks, have very high energy levels, and have a certain amount of control over their lives.

Now, I would like you to think of historical figures. People who you have never met but have a place in history. They could be spiritual leaders, military leaders, philanthropists, heads of state, entrepreneurs, whatever you choose. Ask yourself this question: "Out of all the people—men or women—in history, whom do I have the greatest admiration and respect for?" Who would be number two? Who would be number three?

1.

2.

3.

Now, starting with your first choice—the one person you admire and respect the most in all of mankind's history—ask the same questions you asked for the persons you know in your own life. Would you say he/she had a positive self-image? Was this person confident in their abilities? Was he/she someone who took action or who waited for things to happen to them? Were they committed to something in a positive way? Would you say they liked themselves? Did they take the steps to control their own life or did life generally control them? Did fears, doubts, and anxiety control them, or did they have a positive outlook about themselves and those around them? Did they generally procrastinate, or were they someone who "did it now?" On a scale of 1-10 with 10 being the highest, what was this person's energy level compared to others of their age? Was this number one person on your list passionate about life or lackadaisical and uninterested? Did they care about others? Did they give of themselves to others? Now, go ahead and ask the same questions about each of the others on your list.

Now it's time for you to honestly appraise your beliefs about yourself. Don't be scared because this is what it's all about. Once you identify your limiting beliefs you can easily change them. We'll start with the positive things. List five positive beliefs you have about yourself. These are beliefs that empower you, allow you to grow as a person each day, benefit those around you, and make you happy and at peace with yourself.

1.
2.
3.
4.
5.

Now, list five negative beliefs about yourself. These beliefs limit you and take away from your peace of mind. What are five beliefs about yourself that you would change if you could?

1.
2.
3.
4.
5.

Now, for each of these five negative beliefs I would like you to make a list of a minimum of five ways these beliefs limit you. Make the list as long as you can for each of them, but a minimum of five. How do these beliefs keep you from reaching your life's goals? How could they potentially limit or harm those around you; particularly those you love?

After you have completed this process, make a list of the beliefs you would like to have to replace these limiting beliefs. For each of these new beliefs make a list of at list five benefits you will gain from them. How will these new beliefs make your life better? What positive effects will they have on your life today? How will your new beliefs benefit others; particularly those you love?

What does your future look like one year from now with your new beliefs? Just as in our previous exercises, the clarity of your visualization of your new future accelerates its becoming reality.

Five years from now with your new beliefs?

Ten years from now?

Twenty years from now?

That is your exercise for today. Have fun, and I'll see you tomorrow.

Chapter Twelve

Abe Lincoln and "The Perfect Ten."

Welcome to chapter twelve. Hopefully you identified some limiting beliefs you've been dragging through your life like overstuffed luggage full of old clothes. It's time to get rid of them and get a new wardrobe, don't you agree? You should have also identified some beliefs that empower you. Isn't it an exciting future that awaits you when you adopt these new—empowering—beliefs, and make them your new filter to the outside world?

Perhaps you chose Abraham Lincoln as one of your historical heroes. Whether you did or not, you no doubt would agree that Abe had very empowering beliefs about himself. It may be interesting for you to know that Abe had major obstacles to overcome in his life long before he became the President of the United States. And, even as President—although most Americans believe him to be a hero—a great many Americans of his time reviled him. One of the beliefs that Abe had was that failure was only a very temporary condition. He believed that you only fail when you stop trying. As evidence of this it would be fun to review some of the *successes* that Abe achieved in his life:

1832-Lost job/Defeated for state legislature
1833-Failed in business
1835-Sweetheart died
1836-Had nervous breakdown
1838-Defeated for Illinois House Speaker
1843-Defeated for nomination for Congress

1848-Lost re-nomination for Congress
1849-Rejected for land officer
1854-Defeated for US Senate
1856-Defeated for nomination for Vice President
1858-Again defeated for US Senate
1860-Elected President of the US

Abe Lincoln also had successes in his life, which I haven't recorded here. You can do some research on his life through the Internet or at the library if you want to know more. But the point is a young man who was born in a log cabin from a very poor family, with very limited education until adulthood, worked through all the failures, disappointments, and rejections and became the 16th President of the United States. In many people's minds he is the greatest President the US has ever had. We can learn a lot from his life, his beliefs about himself, and his resiliency as a human being.

One of the personal belief systems it would be wise for you to adopt is that rejection is not a rejection of you as a person—it's a temporary situation. Virtually every person who people look up to as a success has undergone failure and rejection repeated times before they "made it." In fact, most of the time the greatest success occurs just after the greatest disappointment. An old expression you may want to remember is, "The darkest hour is always just before the dawn." Successful people have learned to look at life this way. If you think they are just made differently than you, think again. No one likes rejection. No one likes to fail. People who continually strive to achieve whatever their personal goals are have simply learned to associate rejection differently than those who quit when they first don't succeed, or those you give up before they learn how to win at the game. They don't take it personally—they just learn from it. I believe that this one fact separates the winners from the losers at life more than any other single factor. Every piece of research I have ever read, every biography of winners I have seen, and my own life experience supports this—winners interpret failure differently than losers.

You can look at it another way. The best major league baseball players either strike out, pop out, or are thrown out at first two out of every three times they get up to bat. The average major leaguer makes an out 75% or more of their ups at bat. Although none of them enjoys making an out they have learned to re-frame this failure—make different mental associations—by understanding the law of averages. The Law of Averages states that over time—at least 100 times—at trying anything, you will succeed a certain number of times, and fail a certain number of times. Out of 100 tries, if you succeed 30 of them you are "batting" .300. Another way to express this is that out of every 100 times, you will succeed 30% of them, and fail 70% of them. Successful people have learned to focus on the successes and learn from the failures. A .300 hitter knows that out of every 100 at bats he will get on base 30 times, or on average, out of every 10 at bats he will get on base 3 times. Now, what if this player strikes out 10 times in a row? Certainly he would want to have his coaches look at his form to make sure that he hadn't changed something in his style from when he was successful. But, once that was assured he could look forward to greater success in the next 10 at bats. Maybe the most exciting part of real life is that unlike baseball you get as many swings at the ball as you want to take. You only make an out when you stop trying. You can stand at the plate and keep swinging until you finally hit your home run.

The law of averages never fails. If you learn to look at life this way, you can re-frame the rejection—or failure—by saying to yourself that every time you fail you bring yourself closer to succeeding. This isn't just a mind trick, either—it's fact. This is just one way to turn a negative situation around and find a way to look at it in a positive way. If you flip a coin ten times in a row and they all come up heads you know that the odds are great that in the next 90 flips there will be more tails than heads. By the time you flip the coin 100 times most likely you will have 50 heads and 50 tails. What are your beliefs about yourself?

YOU ONLY STRIKE OUT......
WHEN YOU STOP SWINGING!

Babe Ruth—The Sultan of Swat—is generally considered to be the greatest baseball player in history, and yet he struck out 1,330 times. Do you think he focused on his strikeouts or his home runs? Reggie Jackson struck out 2,597 times in his career—more than anyone else in history, and yet he is in the Hall of Fame and considered one of the top 100 players to ever play the game. When he stepped up to the plate, what do you think he was focusing on—his strikeouts, or his homeruns?

If someone gave you a treasure map that you believed was authentic that showed a fortune in diamonds buried in your back yard, how hard would you look until you finally gave up? Would you go out with a trowel and dig a little bit in the spot where the X showed on the map, or would you begin a major excavation of your property? Most likely you would quickly adopt the attitude that every barrel of dirt you dug up and sifted through brought you that much closer to the treasure. You wouldn't just dig where you thought the X was, either. You'd continue searching and sifting until you found the treasure. That is exactly the attitude that each of us needs to adopt in our own lives. Remember that the only way you fail is when you stop trying. Don't stop digging one shovel full of dirt before you reach your treasure.

Earlier in this chapter we talked about you getting a new wardrobe of beliefs. I have put together what I call "The Perfect Ten" of beliefs. Olympic gymnasts strive for a perfect ten. We judge the appearance of others on a scale of one to ten; with ten being the best. If you're of my generation you no doubt remember the movie "10" with Bo Derek as the perfect ten. Dave Letterman has his top ten list every night. What follows are the "Perfect Ten" beliefs you may want to have as your own. I guarantee that when you adopt these beliefs you cannot fail at life. Remember that you have the ability to adopt whatever beliefs you want to have for yourself. You have already learned how to do that, haven't you? You owe it to yourself, your loved ones, and those around you to be the best you can be. Make these a part of your very being. Remember that your perception of everything around you is based on the filter of your personal beliefs. Try these beliefs on for size. Use the visualization techniques you have learned and picture what your life will be like a year from now with these beliefs determining how you look at the world. Let your mind and body totally relax as you take these beliefs five years into your future. Ten years into the future. Twenty years into the future. Let your mind create the most vivid images for you to savor. What are the colors you see? What are the sounds you hear? What does your world smell like? What does it feel like to know that this new life is your life? Smile to yourself and feel the satisfaction of the life you have created for yourself because of your beliefs.

1. I am a winner (Or, I only fail when I quit trying)
2. I strive for continuous self-improvement
3. I like and love people and therefore people like and love me in return
4. I make new friends easily
5. I am worthy of the love and respect of myself and others
6. I am worthy of all the good things life can give
7. I am a person of action
8. I love my life and live every day with passion
9. I have unique gifts and abilities that can greatly benefit others and myself
10. I am responsible for every event in my life and I therefore am in control of my life

Your assignment for today is to visualize your future with each of these beliefs being an integral part of you. Take yourself to your place of solitude, do your relaxation exercises and say each one to yourself just as it is written—in the first person present tense. Say each one with conviction and belief. As you say it, visualize the future a person with these beliefs will have—your future. Have fun, and I'll see you tomorrow.

CHAPTER THIRTEEN

QUESTIONS THAT HELP YOU FIND JOY AND HAPPINESS IN YOUR LIFE.

Welcome to chapter thirteen. How did your visualizations of the "Perfect Ten" beliefs go? If you received pushback from your subconscious when you affirmatively stated these beliefs that is because your mind doesn't as yet buy in to them. The old way of getting your subconscious to accept new beliefs was to continually make "affirmations" in the first person over and over again. Unfortunately, for many people this process did not work as effectively as they would have liked. A more effective way of forcing your subconscious to accept new beliefs is to combine the affirmations with questions that make your mind answer in a positive way moving you forward towards the new beliefs you desire. To unlock the power you have in your marvelous mind you will need to keep asking yourself the right questions. You ask yourself questions every day, many times a day. If you're like most people you do it without even realizing it. Asking yourself the wrong questions—which most of us do—is devastating to your self-image and your beliefs about yourself.

ARE YOU ASKING YOURSELF CLOSED-LOOP QUESTIONS?

Because of the negativity of the world and the way most of us were raised we learned to ask ourselves closed-loop questions. A closed loop is a circle that just goes around and around without end.

When you ask yourself questions like this, your mind can't come up with a good answer and so it gets frustrated. Frustration is a negative emotion, isn't it? What happens when we think negative thoughts, or feel negative emotions? That's right, more and more negatives come creeping into our minds. In your heart you've likely already believed the truth of this—you know it to be true. So eventually your mind gives you a negative answer, one that harms your self-image and your self-confidence. The logic of this is indisputable if you think about it. If you were to ask this question to a young child—your son or daughter, sister or brother, cousin, or friend: "Why do you always do such stupid things?"—What answer do you think that child's mind would come up with? Initially, since the child doesn't know why he/she does the things they do they won't be able to come up with an answer. But, you see, the human mind is a strange and wonderful thing. Your mind must come up with an answer to any question you ask yourself—it's the nature of human beings. Since the child looks up to you and wants to please you it will start asking itself that question. "Self (Harry, Martha, or whoever), why do you always do such stupid things?" A young child—and most adults for that matter—hasn't had the training you are receiving from this program, and therefore its mind can come up with no satisfactory answer. There really is only one obvious answer to that question if the mind doesn't have the training in how it works. "If I always do stupid things then I must be stupid, right? Of course, right." Since you would never lie to yourself your sub-conscious mind accepts the truth of this without reservation. From that point on whenever the child does something he/she didn't intend to do (have you ever done something you didn't mean to do? —human nature again, isn't it?) he asks himself a new question: "Why do I have to be so stupid?" Once again, a closed loop question. There is no satisfactory answer to this question, is there? The only answer could possibly be, "You just are—stupid, that's all there is to it." This happened to all of us in our lives at one time or another. Our parents, our older brothers or sisters, our Aunts or Uncles, our teachers, or possibly our peers asked us questions, which forced us to start asking ourselves the wrong questions. Questions which not only became habits for the little voice in our minds that is our thoughts, but which also programmed negative self-image and beliefs in our minds.

So, now that you realize and understand how the mind responds to questions, how can you use this to your advantage? Simple. Start asking yourself the right questions. Anything you do for 21 consecutive days becomes a habit. Just as you can replace negative thoughts with positive ones, you can replace the wrong questions with the right ones. Any question, which forces your mind to come up with an answer, which is positive, is a good question. It's even better if you can ask the question in a way that makes your mind come up with something that will be fun for you. Remember that everything we do is to gain pleasure or avoid pain. The prospect of pleasure makes us look forward to things—makes us take action in a forward manner. This is positive, isn't it? A great question to start with then would be, "What questions can I ask myself every morning which will make me feel good, and will have a positive effect on my growth as a human being for the benefit of others and myself?" Make a list of these questions.

Start, if you like, with the "Perfect Ten" beliefs. Take each belief from the previous chapter and develop a question that will force your mind to eventually accept that belief. If your mind currently argues with you when you make the affirmation it may be because of the negative programming from your youth. It is also possible that you are living your life currently in such a way that contradicts the truth of the belief you are trying to make your own. If that's the case, then some changes in your life must take place. There has to be congruity between our day to day actions and our beliefs. A lack of congruity between our beliefs and our actions causes stress and anxiety. These are negative emotions we want to eliminate from our lives. Hopefully, you agree that the "Perfect Ten" are empowering beliefs that you would like to have. If that's true, then the changes must be made in your daily behavior so that your actions harmonize with your desired beliefs.

START ASKING THE RIGHT QUESTIONS..

As an example of this, let's take belief number five; *I am worthy of the love and respect of others.* If your subconscious pushes back when you state this affirmation, then ask yourself the question, "What can I do today that I will enjoy and that will make me feel worthy of the love and respect of others?" Remember that your mind will always search until it comes up with the right answer to any positively asked question. Don't force your mind to give you the answer immediately—if it does, great. But if it doesn't, have faith that before long the answer will come to you in a flash of truth. The answer will come completely and in a way that you'll know is right.

Another example would be for belief number seven; *I am a person of action.* Ask yourself the question, "What can I do today to develop the habit of taking action, for the benefit of others and myself while enjoying the process?" That's your assignment for today. Make up at least one question for each of the "Perfect Ten." Have fun, and I'll see you tomorrow.

CHAPTER FOURTEEN

ANXIETY, STRESS, AND FIVE FOR TEN

Welcome to chapter fourteen. Did you complete your questions from chapter thirteen? Remember to ask yourself these questions as often as you can all day long. When your mind gives you the answers, make sure you write them down immediately before you forget them. If you don't act on the answers your subconscious gives you it will stop giving you the answers. Action is always the key to success.

DO YOU EVER FEEL LIKE THIS?

We've already spent considerable time discussing what a toll anxiety and stress can take on your life. I really believe that in our modern world these two negative emotions may take a greater toll on our happiness, and cause more health problems than almost anything else. I just read an article, which supports a theory I've been working on about the world we live in today. The headline read "Upheaval increases suicides in Japan;" with a subheading of "People are killing themselves in record numbers. Experts blame the recession." Quoting the article: "Police recently found 73 bodies in the Aokigahara woods, a favorite place for suicides, nestled at the foot of Mount Fuji." The article went on to say that it is not unusual to find bodies here, what's different is the number. About 90 people a day killed themselves last year in Japan, a 34.7 percent rise from the previous year. The blame is being laid at the feet of the cultural shift from one of lifetime employment to the capitalist approach of corporate downsizing in an effort to cut costs, increase profit, and please the shareholders. What the Japanese find particularly disturbing is the increase of 44.6% in suicides of men aged 40-59. Also, 40 percent more men in their 20's killed themselves compared to the year before. Traditionally the 20's were a stable time in Japanese life where young men could count on becoming shaiin, literally "members of society," by entering the workforce. Now, jobs are harder to find. Atsushi Murayama, managing director in charge of personnel at Matsushita Electric Industrial Co. (Panasonic in the US) said, "Of course there is a relationship between restructuring and suicide."

Even having a job doesn't help that much because of people's fear of being one of the next to go when the next downsizing comes around. Having been through these traumas several times in my own career I can personally attest to the stress and anxiety inherent in the corporate culture today. Of course, the men or women experiencing this work related anxiety are not the only ones to experience it, as their wives, husbands, or significant others and their families also feel a great deal of the same stresses. Life today is much more stressful and anxiety ridden than it used to be. "Road Rage" is a phenomenon I never heard of years ago, but today it is very common. In Orlando it is not unusual to hear of someone pulling a gun and shooting someone for cutting him or her off, or committing some type of driving aggression that the other motorist considers inexcusable.

I have to confess that there are times where I find it very difficult to think positive thoughts and experience positive emotions when stuck in traffic on Interstate 4. Pagers, cell phones, voice mail, email; the list goes on and on of the devices that make it more difficult for us to find solace in the world we live in.

If you have ever experienced an anxiety attack you certainly are not alone. It's becoming more difficult to find people, who have never experienced a level of anxiety where they felt like they were losing control, than to find those who have. Behavioral Scientists believe that there is only so much stress and anxiety that the human body can take before it explodes into some form of release that can be extremely damaging to the individual. An example for you to think about here is a drip bucket you may have used at some point to hold the water from a leak in your ceiling or from your plumbing. The water accumulates very slowly doesn't it? Drip by little drip the water accumulates. At some point the water spills out of the bucket, but the accumulation is so slow it's difficult for you to determine when the spillover occurs. Anxiety and stress is just like the drips going into the drip bucket. You are probably aware that stress can contribute to high blood pressure, hardening of the arteries, heart disease, headaches, tension in the neck, nervousness and other common maladies. Recently stress has been attributed to chronic back pain—especially lower back pain, uncontrollable shaking of the extremities, lowering of the body's auto-immune system, and can even simulate a heart attack—right down to the numbness of the arms and legs. In *Is It Worth Dying For?* Dr. Robert Eliot attributes the "fight or flight" reaction, which triggers most if not all panic attacks to stress. Stress stimulates two responses in the body which cause this:

1. An acute alarm reaction which prepares the body for flight
2. A "chronic vigilance" reaction which prepares the body for long-term endurance

FIGHT!.....OR, FLIGHT?

Adrenaline races through the body, commanding a series of physical changes: the heart beats faster and stronger so blood pressure rises abruptly. Automatically, blood is shunted away from the stomach and skin, where it is not needed, to the muscles, where it is; high–energy fats are rushed into the bloodstream for energy. Chemicals are released to make the blood clot more quickly in case of injury. The nerves cause the pupils to dilate; the facial muscles tense, blood vessels in the skin open up and the face flushes, the breathing quickens, and blood sugar increases. You're ready for physical action. If this happens to you while you're in a crowded restaurant or on a date it can obviously be somewhat disconcerting, because your body takes over and you want to flee the scene. This "fight or flight" reaction is what triggers the first event for agoraphobics who develop a paralyzing fear of leaving their home, even to go out for groceries or to visit a friend. We know that without understanding the cause of this event the individual can begin to associate this humiliating sense of loss of control to almost any place, or circumstance in their lives. As we've discussed; in many cases just the understanding of what caused the initial event, combined with relaxation and positive visualization techniques can be a permanent cure to this debilitating phobia.

Regardless of the level your stress and anxiety has reached in your life it is clear that to gain peace of mind on the level we would all like to have we must learn to manage stress better. Once again, the answer comes with controlling our mental states, or state of mind. We've shown you ways to re-associate a past negative event with a positive thought and hence positive emotions. The questions you've hopefully learned by now that you can ask yourself every day to experience more positive emotions in your life can greatly reduce your stress level, and help you to enjoy your life to a greater extent. You owe it to yourself and those around you—particularly those you love—to manage your stress. The easiest way to do this is by simply asking yourself, "What positive lesson can I learn from this event that will help me look at a similar event differently the next time it occurs?" By asking yourself this question—or a similar positively phrased one—you allow your subconscious mind to give you an answer which will give you more positive emotions. You are making new mental associations—positive, empowering ones. Remember that every time you turn a potential negative experience—thought or emotion—into a positive one, you release more of the brakes, which hold you back from being the person you want to be. The glue on the flypaper of negativism gets weaker and weaker every time you do this.

When you were growing up your mother or father probably told you to count your blessings. You may have never understood what that meant, or you got so tired of hearing it you decided when you grew up you'd never do it again. They may have told you this when you complained you didn't have the same toy that Johnny or Mary up the street had just gotten. According to what I read the children today have more material things than at any time in history. I know when I was in school we never cared—I'm a guy, remember—what kind of clothes we had. Today, in many schools the kids without the right clothes are ridiculed and outcast like they have some kind of communicable disease. I'll never forget the night my thirteen year old son banged his head against the wall in his bedroom as he cried uncontrollably—my wife and I thought he'd lost his mind. All of this was brought on we found because he was being picked on at school for not having the "in" clothes.

IS IT WORTH IT?

It seems that every day there is a new stress thrown at us. Let's face it; it's a very negative world. The nightly newscasts are filled with tales of war atrocities, one race hating another race, ethnic cleansing, violence in the schools, somebody getting shot, raped, stabbed, or all of the above. All of this negative data gets thrown at us daily. You might legitimately ask, "Okay, Dennis, you keep telling me to think positive thoughts and allow positive emotions to replace negative ones. How do I do this when all I hear is negative?" You ask a good question. My answer goes back to what your parents told you when you were growing up. It's the same thing I say constantly to my own three children. "Count your blessings." It's been said so many times for so many years that it's become one of those old trite clichés. But let me ask you this: If you count your blessings every day, what effect does that have on your mental state? Is it positive or negative? Try something on for the next ten days and see how you like it. Make believe that your favorite clothing store let you buy a new wardrobe for ten days with a money back guarantee. If you don't like it after ten days just bring it back. If you don't feel this is beneficial to your life and your sense of well being after trying it for ten days; don't do it anymore. But, if you really like it, I want you to keep it, okay? In other words keep on doing it until it becomes a habit. I call this the "five for ten"—kind of a play on words from the days when we had five and dime stores. For the next ten days, ask yourself these five questions every morning as soon as you wake up and every night just before you go to bed. The morning questions will allow your subconscious to give you all the positive emotions that go along with these blessings all day long. The nighttime questions will allow your subconscious to re-program itself with positive thoughts and emotions while you sleep.

1. Who do I love and who loves me?
2. What one thing about myself do I really like? Or, what am I most proud of in my life right now?
3. What three things in my life right now do I get the most joy from?
4. What can I do today to have some fun? The nighttime question will be "What can I do tomorrow to have some fun?
5. What can I do today/tomorrow to bring joy to someone else?

That's your assignment for today and tomorrow morning. Have fun. I'll see you tomorrow.

Chapter Fifteen

Phobias and anxiety disorder

Welcome to chapter fifteen. Did you ask yourself the "Five for Ten" questions last night and this morning? Did you experience the positive emotions from your asking yourself the right type of questions? If you did, wouldn't you like to experience these positive emotions every night and every morning? Remember that the more our minds are allowed to dwell on the positives, the less our natural inclinations will be to look at the negatives in our lives. The negatives will find us without our help, won't they? All we have to do is go to work or turn on the news and we'll quickly get all the negatives we could ever ask for, isn't that true? While you're training your mind to focus on the sunny side it might be good for you to begin to think about the people you associate with on a regular basis. Are you getting a regular dose of negativism from your friends? How about your family? The more you allow yourself to be exposed to negativism the harder it will be to create the positive habits you desire.

WHICH DRIP SPILLS YOUR BUCKET?

If you have suffered from anxiety and panic attacks, or any kind of phobia, you know it is a very serious matter. It has been estimated that more than 10% of the population suffers from one or more of these disorders. In my research I was amazed by these statistics, but not totally surprised, as most people do not understand what causes their fears, and anxieties. In the book *The Encyclopedia Of Phobias, Fears, and Anxieties* there are over 2,000 entries, most of these labeling different types of phobias. Probably the most serious type of phobia is agoraphobia—fear of leaving a safe place. Most agoraphobics commonly fear going away from home, going into the street, into stores, occupying center seats in church or movie theatres, public transportation, crowded places, and anyplace where there are crowds of people gathered. This phobia normally begins with a panic experience followed by extreme sensitivity to bodily sensations, self-judgment, helplessness, and social anxiety. Most agoraphobics develop additional phobias as their cycle of fear and helplessness grows. The panic experience can be caused initially by many factors. Specific foods and medications can contribute to it; such as caffeine, pseudophedrine that is found in many over-the-counter cold and allergy medicines, diet pills, and most illicit drugs. Marijuana is associated with many initial panic attacks.

I would imagine that unless you skipped right to this chapter because you suffer from these disorders you have already analyzed and understood the causes of your attacks and may have already overcome them. The exercises we have practiced on relaxation, positive visualization, and learning to form new positive mental associations to past events is key to eliminating your phobias. As we've said, almost all phobias start with an event which can be caused by some real trauma or pain, but for the most part is triggered by a build up of too much anxiety from the stresses of life. In the chapter on *Anxiety and Stress* we talked about the drip bucket you may have used at some point to hold the water from a leak in your ceiling or from your plumbing. The water accumulates so slowly that if you stand there watching it you can't notice the gradual changes in the water level. Drip by little drip the water accumulates. At some point the water spills out of the bucket, but the accumulation is so slow it's difficult for you to determine when the

spillover occurs. Anxiety and stress is just like the drips going into the drip bucket. We live in a very stressful world, don't we? I know from personal experience that the anxieties from career and/or home-life can spillover your bucket without you even being consciously aware of the level reaching the top. You may not even be aware of the cause of the anxiety—but it's there. But, when that last drip of anxiety hits the bucket all of a sudden an attack ensues. Rising heart rate, rising blood pressure and an incredible desire to escape can take over, seemingly without cause.

The original pain or trauma is so disconcerting that very quickly the phobia is no longer a fear of any particular thing, but really a fear of fear. We have said repeatedly in the pages of this book that any individual is happy and at peace with themselves to the exact degree that they are in control of their own lives. The panic that envelops you if you have these disorders is caused for exactly the reason that you feel your life is out of your control. Understanding the cause of the fear and changing your mental focus from the fear to the

positive future you will enjoy without the fear is the cure. It's that simple and easy. The key to overcoming your phobia is to understand that the fear isn't real. Remember Paul Atreides in Dune from Chapter Two? Nothing will really happen to you. You won't go crazy, you won't jump out of the window, and you won't harm yourself or others. Just keep telling yourself it's frightening, but it's not dangerous. It's going to pass. Melvin Green, director of an agency that treats agoraphobia, likens the attack to a small wave that can be seen approaching a beach. As the wave approaches land it grows larger and larger. This represents your feelings of anxiety growing. Soon the wave is very large and peaks. It then flows down into smaller and smaller waves until it eventually disperses on the beach. Flow with your feelings as you would with the wave on the beach. Eventually it will subside. The key thing to remember is that it won't harm you. Something that has helped me was to remind myself that no matter how much others may appear to have it all together, no one really does. This realization was a revelation for me. Once I realized that everyone is just trying to figure it all out I began to blossom as a human being. You are not alone, I assure you.

THE WAVES OF PANIC WILL GRADUALLY DECREASE UNTIL THEY DISAPPEAR.

Concentrating on your breathing may also help you. Panic attacks cause many to hyperventilate. It may help to reduce the intensity of the attack if you inhale and breathe slowly, especially by breathing through the nose instead of the mouth. Learn to breathe from the diaphragm instead of the upper chest. While standing up; test yourself by placing one hand above your waist and the other in the middle of your chest. While you breathe notice which hand is moving more. If it is the hand on your chest you are not breathing from your diaphragm. You will need to practice your slow, deep, diaphragm breathing techniques remembering that the normal ratio of diaphragm-to-chest breaths is about 4 to 1. Those with chronic respiratory conditions—such as emphysema or asthma—should see your doctor before attempting new breathing techniques.

If you did go right to this chapter you will need to go back to the chapter entitled *Understanding Fear*? As we discussed in that chapter, your mind has formed numerous associations to your original attack, which must be changed. You must change it and look beyond your fear, not at your fear. This is somewhat like saying, "Don't think of pink elephants," isn't it? That is why you will need to interrupt your anxiety pattern. Sing a song, jump on one leg, snap a rubber band on your wrist, or count backward from thirty. Focus your mind on something other than the fear. By continually focusing on your fear it becomes greater and greater. Some have had success playing a little game with their fear, such as making believe the scary mental image is being viewed through a camera lens which can adjust the size, distance, even color of the image. Make the image move farther and farther away until it is so small you can barely see it. You can make it disappear entirely if you want to. Change the mental image into something humorous or entirely unthreatening for you. Remember that this fear doesn't really exist anyway—it's all in your mind. There are no rules that say you can't make a mental game out of a purely mental process. It's your mind, isn't it? You can make up your own rules as long as they advantage you. If you learn to have fun with it you replace negative thoughts and emotions with positive ones. Remember that you can't feel a positive emotion and a negative emotion at the same time—the switch is either on or off, it can't be both. Ask yourself the question, "How can I have some fun with this?" Remember that your mind will always give you the right answer to a positively asked question.

We have spent considerable time discussing focusing your mind on positive outcomes through visualization techniques. We have also discussed anchoring your thoughts to a positive reference point different from your fear. Robert Handly, in his book written with Pauline Neff, entitled *Anxiety & Panic Attacks—Their Cause And Cure*—talks about changing his outlook on his own agoraphobia to a positive one. He has learned to re-associate—re-frame—a past negative event by thinking of his phobia as the great motivator for positive change in his life. We've spent many pages in this book talking about learning to ask yourself the right questions. A great question to ask yourself is "In what ways can I use my fear as a positive driving force to eliminate the negative emotions and thoughts in my life for the benefit of others and myself while enjoying the process?"

Go back and review the chapter *What is Love.* What negative emotions are controlling you? Learn to think happy thoughts and to visualize positive outcomes in your life. Read the chapter *Happy Thoughts.* Practice it. As we discussed in the chapter *Understanding Fear,* you are the one who controls your thoughts—no one else. Make a list of your fears and how they are damaging you. Drag these fears with you into the future 5, 10, 15, and 20 years while visualizing what your life will be like if you don't change now. Once this is done allow yourself the joy of—just for the moment—experiencing true peace and joy. Think of a time and a place in your life where you were totally at peace with yourself. If nothing comes to your mind then allow yourself to think of a place where you think you'd find complete peace and joy. While in this mental state take yourself into the future 5 years without any of your fears. How do you feel? Now take yourself—without your fears—10 years into the future. Allow your mind the pleasure of making your fantasy as vivid as you can make it. See the colors; see the happy faces of your loved ones smiling as they enjoy the you without fear. Smell the smells, feel the joy of the you without fear. Take the new you 20 years into the future. What is the you without fear doing? Who are there with you? Allow yourself the pleasure of seeing the joy in their eyes, and the smiles on their faces. How does it feel to know you have no fears controlling your life?

Once you've practiced these mental exercises, challenge yourself to face your fear. While in a state of total relaxation take yourself mentally into one of the places where you would normally experience increased anxiety. Allow yourself the joy of knowing that you have conquered your fear. See yourself smiling after successfully doing something that the old you—the one controlled by fear—wouldn't have done. Allow yourself the satisfaction of feeling proud of you. Thousands of others have used these methods successfully and have overcome their fears. You can, too.

TAKE BABY STEPS...

Don't be angry with yourself if you don't reach your ultimate goal right away. Anger, guilt, and frustration are negative emotions, which cling like flypaper to other negative emotions. Allow yourself the luxury of only positive thoughts and the positive feelings that go with them. Don't be afraid to take "baby steps" towards becoming the person you desire to be. As long as you continue setting new incremental goals for yourself—baby steps—towards becoming the person you want to be you're making positive progress. Baby steps can have great power. The book you are reading is the result of many many baby steps. I didn't sit down one day and write a book—it doesn't work that way. First an idea comes into your mind, then a very rough structure of what chapters you might want to include, and then you put some of your thoughts down on paper—or word processor.

It is a very gradual process, but eventually if you keep plugging at it you reach your goal. Every baby learns to walk eventually, but rarely do they just get up one day and walk across the room. Strive for incremental improvements every day and eventually you'll end up where you want to be. Remember that termites cause more property damage than all earthquakes, tornadoes, and hurricanes combined. These tiny insects eating just a little wood at a time will eventually destroy your entire home if left unchecked. Great successes happen by a series of little steps taken in the right direction. Allow yourself the joy of taking pride in every baby step you take.

Your exercise for today is to go through your visualization exercises described above for at least 20 minutes or so. Then, take one positive action towards overcoming your fear. You decide how big or small those steps will be. Remember that you have to begin a journey before you can ever reach the destination. Start your journey to becoming the new you today. Have fun, and I'll see you tomorrow.

Chapter Sixteen

What is success?

Welcome to chapter sixteen. How did it feel yesterday to face your fear? Didn't it give you a feeling of satisfaction? Congratulations, you're well on your way to becoming the person you want to be.

Are you successful? Believe it or not, almost every person has a different definition for success. If your answer was no, how do you know you aren't? Without even knowing you I'm willing to bet that there are people who would consider you successful. Is a millionaire successful in your opinion? How about Bill Gates, is he successful? Is a woman who doesn't work outside the home, but finds total satisfaction caring for her family successful? What would you say about Hillary Clinton? Is she successful? Why do you say that?

Is she successful?

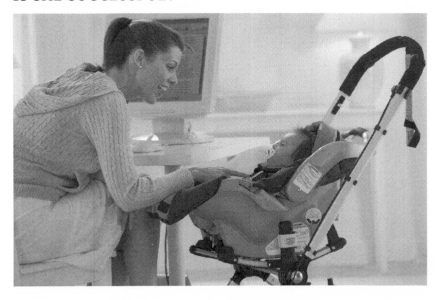

What is your definition of success? Go ahead and write it down, I'll wait.

One definition for success that I've heard is this: *Success is the realization of a worthy goal.*
Would you agree with this definition?
Another definition I've heard has six components to it. They include:

1. Regularly experiencing positive emotions (Love, joy, peace, etc.) and freedom from negative emotions such as fear, doubt, and worry.
2. Worthy goals and ideals
3. High levels of health and energy
4. Loving relationships
5. Freedom from financial concerns
6. Feeling of personal fulfillment

If your life matched the six criteria above would you be successful? There's no question that once you have excelled in each of these six areas you'll be doing very well. The only problem that I have with this definition is that it's pretty tough to get there. I want my self-fulfillment now. I want to feel good about myself now.

Success is not a destination any more than life is a destination. You no doubt have heard the old saying, "Life is what happens to you while you're busy making other plans." Isn't that really true for almost all of us? If you put too strict a definition on success then what do you do when you get there? I believe that success is a journey just as is life. If you think about the Universe, including the galaxies, stars, and planets, everything is in a state of movement and constant change. We know that the Universe is expanding. Scientists believe that at some point in the distant past there was a "Big Bang" where incredible amounts of energy (Einstein's theory of relativity) converted to matter and the Universe was born. Whether you believe this to be an act of Creation, or an event of miraculous happenstance, we know that it happened. If we think for a moment about our own solar system we know that the planets are all spinning on their axis, while at the same time traveling at incredible speeds in their orbits around our sun, which is itself moving within the Milky Way galaxy, which itself is moving. Our moon rotates around the earth, while the earth rotates on it's own axis once every 24 hours. On our planet earth—the only place in the Universe where we know life exists—there is incredible abundance of life. From viruses, amoebas, and other life forms that we need powerful microscopes to even see, to the highest life form on the planet—you—everything is in a constant state of change, isn't it? Life is either being born or its dying. You are either growing up, or you're getting older. You're either getting fatter or you're getting thinner. You're both gaining knowledge and skills through a conscious effort on your part to improve yourself, or you're forgetting things you once knew because of lack of practice and getting older. Every human being is in a constant state of becoming. You're either becoming better as a human being because of a conscious plan you have made and regular consistent effort to follow it, or you're becoming worse because of the negative influences which are abundant around us. What is happening without you even being aware of it is that you are changing in the direction of your dominant thoughts. Whatever you think about on a regular basis is what you are moving towards—becoming. This happens whether you want it to or not. Your mind is like a garden. If you don't continually tend it, feed it the right nutrients and water it, before you know it it's full of weeds. Weeds, as we know, suck the life away from the flowers, vegetables or whatever it is we want to grow.

EVERYTHING IN CONSTANT MOTION..

Hopefully you agree that if you're constantly changing anyway, it makes sense to change in the direction of positive growth. My personal definition of success is: "Asking myself the right questions every day to experience more positive emotions for the benefit of others and myself and having fun doing it." If you adopt my definition of success you can be successful **today** can't you? The whole idea is feeling good about yourself now—not some undetermined time in the future—and growing as a person while doing it. Remember that if you're not growing you're dying. If we don't continue the process of personal growth we begin to regress. You've begun a process that you'll continue for the rest of your life. Fortunately you have now developed the right habits. But, I caution you, just as bad habits can be changed, so can good habits. It's important that you allow yourself the luxury of associating with people who also are on a mission of self-improvement. Surround yourself with positive people, with positive goals. Feed your mind positive thoughts every day. Keep the process going in the right direction.

I have another question for you. Are you happy? We've agreed that happiness is a state of mind. We discussed earlier that any of us can be happy at any time just by thinking happy thoughts—remember Peter Pan. Unfortunately, though, we don't live in a very happy world. Every time we turn on the news or pick up the newspaper we are exposed to a great deal of unhappiness. In fact, many feel that the media couldn't survive if it weren't for human misery. Even though we'd like to be able to think happy thoughts all the time it is pretty much impossible. The world around us is a pretty negative place. You no doubt knew before you ever bought this book that it was good to be positive. Everyone knows that thinking positive is beneficial, but few do it. So, what is the solution? If everyone wants to be happy and we're all bombarded every day by unhappiness what can we do about it? Again, we have to continually look for positive material to feed our minds, and continue to ask ourselves the right questions. Happiness—just like life and success—is not a destination at all, it is a process. It's a by-product of living a fruitful life. Happiness comes to us, not when we strive for it, but when we strive to become better persons every day of our lives, for the benefit of others and ourselves.

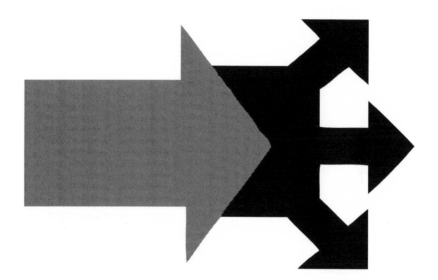

Are you headed in the RIGHT direction?

Your assignment for today is to make a list of six questions to ask yourself several times a day. Each question should be designed to make your mind—and your life—take the direction towards the attainment of one of the six parts of the success definition above. These questions must be asked in the first person—I, and take you in a positive direction for self-improvement. In order for your subconscious mind to give you the right answers to your questions they must be asked in a positive way and not be at the expense of any other person. In fact, if other people can be benefited at the same time so much the better. The question should include a "How do I," or "What can I," or "In what ways can I." The question should also be asked so that whatever answer comes back will be acted on today, or right now. Each question should also include "while enjoying the process," or "having fun doing it." For example, item number six is

111

"self fulfillment." A good question to ask yourself each day would be *"What can I do today to gain a greater feeling of personal fulfillment in my life for the benefit of others and myself while having fun doing it?"* I only write this as an example. It would be better if you would write your own. Once you have created these six questions start asking yourself these questions today. Set a goal to make this process a good habit that you will have to make a conscious mental effort to change. The little voice in your mind that is your thoughts will take over once the habit is a part of you. Your doing the same thing every day for at least 21 consecutive days makes it become a habit.

1.
2.
3.
4.
5.
6.

Remember that your subconscious mind may not give you the answer immediately. Don't try to force the answers with conscious thought. Remember that mental processes work the best when you completely relax. Frustration results when you push your mind, resulting in negative emotions, which scares the positive answers away. Ask the questions of yourself with the belief that your mind will give you the perfect answers when it wants to. Just keep asking the right questions. When the right answers come you will know it. Trust yourself. Have fun. I'll see you tomorrow.

Chapter Seventeen

Career Planning

Welcome to chapter seventeen. How did you do with your six questions? You should be noticing by now that your mind is re-programming to think positively and that without even thinking about it consciously you are asking yourself questions that help you to look at life in a much more beneficial way for your happiness and personal growth. To continue on this positive road you will need to get yourself in the right daily pursuits that you enjoy while working for the benefit of others and yourself. It's pretty tough to be positive if your job or daily routine is unfulfilling—or worse. I don't believe that anyone should have to go through life doing a job that they despise. What a waste. You have gifts that are unique and special to you. Nobody else on this planet has the same experiences and talents as you—nobody. You can make a difference. A hundred years from now what legacy will you have left?

WHAT'S YOUR ONE THING?

The first step anyone should take in deciding what their main occupation in life should be is to determine the thing they most enjoy doing. It isn't "rocket science," as they say, to understand that we generally do the best at things that we really enjoy doing. Or, maybe we really enjoy doing the things that we naturally do well. I'm not sure which is the chicken and which is the egg here. Everyone has unique talents and abilities. Some of us have gifts in speaking, others have high mechanical aptitudes. Others may have athletic talents, or the ability to teach. No matter who you are you have a unique gift/gifts in certain areas.

If you think about your own life, isn't it true that if you have something planned for the day that you really enjoy, you jump out of bed with an enthusiasm that you might not normally have? I've often heard that the way to plan a career is to find the one thing in our lives that we enjoy so much we would do it for free, and then find a way to make money at it. It's obvious to me that if you have a passion for something it will be easier to put in the effort that any successful pursuit normally requires. We've all seen the Biographies of famous, successful people, and the sacrifices they made to "get to the top." Just recently my family was watching the story of the Judd family—Naomi and Wynona, the famous country music singers. I happened to catch some of it on TV, and I couldn't help but think that many people think success just falls into people's laps. If you know anything about the Judds, you know it didn't happen that way for them. Those who have spent the time analyzing how success happens know that it almost never works that way. Interestingly enough, when it does happen that way there is normally a reversal of fortune where the career takes a steep nose-dive, either because the success was accidental, or the person wasn't mentally prepared for it.

Tony Robbins talks about his first rise to stardom where he was called "The Wonderboy." Without really understanding why or how, he became famous and wealthy at a very young age giving seminars on personal development. Because he didn't fully understand why he was doing so well, and hadn't reconciled his self-image with his new found fortune he began to sabotage himself and soon lost it all. He had to truly understand himself, re-define his beliefs about himself, and then re-build his success. Of course, we know that he was able to do that and is extremely successful today—far more than the first time around. But, one of the reasons—maybe the biggest reason—Tony has been so incredibly successful is that he absolutely loves doing what he does. He was one of those rare individuals who was fortunate enough to be able to identify his life's calling at an early enough age and then plan a career around it.

Investing works much the same way. If you're planning for retirement, the earlier you start the easier it will be to amass a fortune later on in life. Why? Because of compound interest, the greater the amount of time for the money to grow, the greater the fortune. If you were to take a penny and double it you now have two cents—not a lot of money. But if you were to double that penny just thirty times you'd have several million dollars. If you don't believe me try it yourself. If someone who is 20 years old invests $2000 in a 401K or IRA account and continues to invest only $2000 each year for 40 years, they will have accumulated $1,928,719 by the time they reach 60, if the annual return averages only 12%. The entire stock market has averaged at least that for the last thirty years, so this is not an unusually high rate of return. The key is starting early and being consistent in your approach.

Although this chapter wasn't written as a seminar on retirement planning, the point is the same. The earlier you make your plan and work your plan the greater your success will be over time. You might ask: "If it's so easy to build a retirement then why do less than 5% of people have financial independence when they reach retirement? The answer is simple. Most people don't start early enough. Most people don't start planning for retirement until they get close enough to it where it becomes a priority. Life planning works the same way. Most of us only wake up when we have a "mid-life crisis" and realize that the years ahead of us are quickly becoming fewer than the years behind us, and that we're stuck in a life that we really didn't plan and don't really want. If you are young enough where this doesn't apply to you, congratulations. As they say, "Your whole life is ahead of you." Don't wait until your life fits the description above and then decide you want to plan your goals and your life. Do it now! The earlier you start, the better your results, and the richer your life will be.

But don't despair if you are not in your 20's or even in your 30's—it's never to late to start planning your life, just as it's never too late to start an investment portfolio. You may have less time for your plan to take effect but you also have experience that you didn't have when you were younger. Michael Jordan was just as effective—some say more so—in his last years as a basketball player than he was in his early years. What he had lost in athletic ability he more than made up for with his mind—his experience of the game. In your case, it's an even better deal. Unless your dream career requires the physical attributes of someone in their teens or

20's, the only thing you've wasted is the time. You don't need the athletic skills of a young person to pursue most of the careers people dream about. John F. Kennedy was the youngest President to ever hold office, and he was in his 40's. Most Presidents are in their 50's, 60's, or even 70's. Colonel Sanders didn't start his Kentucky Fried Chicken business until his early 70's. Zig Ziglar was a failure—in his words—until his 40's.

You also don't necessarily need a background in the career choice you identify. An example of someone who made a dramatic career change is Jessie Ventura. Who would have ever thought that a professional wrestler would become Governor of Minnesota? Of course, there are some realities that we need to consider, here. If you're 45, and you've just realized that your real dream is to be a professional football quarterback, it's probably too late. But, if your true passion is professional football, is there some other career that would allow you to be an integral part of the game? Could you coach? Could you become an agent? Could you get involved in the management of a team somehow? Could you become a sports announcer, or a sports reporter? Could you become an owner of a team? Remember that asking yourself the right questions will always provide the right answers. If you can't figure out a way to become involved in the professional game, would it be just as fulfilling—or maybe more so—to get involved at the college level in some way, or maybe the high school or grade school level. There's always a way if we're willing to open up our minds and keep asking the right questions.

If your true passion is unavailable to you as a way to make money, would it be just as enjoyable—or more so—to do volunteer work that will use your gifts only for the benefit of others? Even though this is a chapter on career planning, it's really your life you're planning, isn't it? Remember my definition of success? Asking myself the right questions every day to experience more positive emotions for the benefit of others and myself and having fun doing it. The positive emotions you'll experience by giving of yourself without thought of yourself will open entirely new avenues in your life that maybe you hadn't even considered.

Maybe you're in the position of life where you are supporting a family with your current job, or career, and can't change. Do you enjoy what you're doing? If not, is there a way for you to move towards a different position with your current employer where you would enjoy your job? Is there something about your current job that is causing you to not enjoy it that could be changed? Even though I would like to know you personally to help you find the right direction for your life, I can't do that. But if you ask yourself the right questions, you will come up with the answers to take your life in the direction you want it to go. The real key is not to give up on yourself or on your life. It's your life. Don't waste it. Have you ever seen the movie *City Slickers* with Billy Crystal? Billy Crystal and two of his city-slicker buddies are all going through a midlife crisis. They take a "vacation" by becoming cowboys, where they have to drive a herd of cattle across the state. The vacation turns out to be anything but, but all of them are forever changed by the experience. There's a scene where the real cowhand—Curly, played by Jack Palance—holds up his index finger and tells the Billy Crystal character that life is all about "one thing." Billy Crystal at first can't understand what Curly is talking about but later understands that he's saying that each of us has one thing in our lives that really matters. "Find out what that 'one thing' is," says Curly, "and you will have it all." What "one thing" have you always wanted to do?

WHAT IS YOUR "ONE" THING?

Your assignment for today is to brainstorm with yourself what careers, hobbies or volunteer work will give your life richness and joy. The key to successful brainstorming is not to judge whether your thoughts are right or wrong—write them all down. Everything that pops into your mind should be written down. Write as fast as you can without judging the merits of the idea. You can always go back later and delete the ideas that don't make sense for you. Remember that—as we've said many times in this book—the key to consistent happiness in our lives is the removal of all negative emotions. Being judgmental is one type of negative emotion. Any negative will scare away the positive ideas your subconscious wants to give you. Let whatever comes to you flow freely onto the paper. I've put ten numbers down but don't be limited to that—the more ideas you write the better. Today you will want to write it all down. Go ahead and have fun with it.

1.
2.
3.
4.
5.
6.
7.
8.
9.
10.

Now go back and sift through—like panning for gold—for the true gem/gems you've written. Go through the list you've just made and narrow it down to the top three.

Now do the "Curly" analysis. Which one of the ten or more things you've written is your one thing? Start asking yourself the right questions, such as, "What are the ways I can take my life in the direction of the one area that would give my life joy and personal fulfillment?" Make an action plan.

Step One:

Step Two:

Step Three:

Step Four, Five, Six, etc:

Make as detailed a plan of action as you can. What can you do today to start the journey to your desired destination? Remember that winners take action. You're a winner, aren't you? Take action for your new future today. Have fun, and I'll see you tomorrow.

CHAPTER EIGHTEEN

GOAL SETTING

Welcome to chapter eighteen. How did your brainstorming go? Were you able to identify what your "one" thing is? Hopefully, you have started your action plan to realize your dream. Congratulations. Of course, your career is just one aspect of your life. What about everything else?

WITHOUT A MAP, WOULD YOU KNOW WHERE YOU'RE GOING?

If you were just to jump in your car and start driving where would you end up? Without planning a destination and getting directions and a road map you could end up anywhere. My Dad used to say, "You only get one walk through this veil of tears so you better make the most of it, and enjoy it." I'm sure that he didn't make it up but I can honestly say I've never heard it said exactly that way anywhere else.

No doubt you have been on at least one vacation in your life where you took a trip somewhere. Maybe you only had a week or two that you could take off from work or away from whatever your normal duties were so you took the time to plan it carefully. I know people who have been so busy on their vacation they couldn't wait to get back to work so they could get some rest. If you plan a vacation carefully so that it turns out well, shouldn't you take the time to plan your life? The average life span still ends somewhere in the 70's regardless of improved knowledge of nutrition and advances in medicine. You've probably already realized how quickly the years fly by—I know I have. Most people never take the time to plan what they want to accomplish in their lives, the places they want to see, or the variety of experiences they want to have. Most of us plan more for the type of dress or suit we want at the store than we take to think about the qualities we really need or want in a wife, husband, or significant other. Even fewer still take the time to write these things down. It doesn't make a lot of sense does it? When you go to the grocery store chances are you take the time to make a list of everything you need to buy. "Honey do lists" are a standing joke for husbands who finally get a holiday from work. Almost all the business people I know have some type of daily planner where they write the tasks that need to be done that day. Chances are you do the same thing. When something is important we take the time to write it down so we don't forget to do it, or buy it.

WHEN IT'S IMPORTANT WE WRITE IT DOWN..

How would you feel if the next time you get on an airplane, just before take-off the pilot announces, "Ladies and gentlemen, welcome aboard, we don't really know where we're going or when we'll arrive but the weather looks fine so it should be a smooth flight, enjoy the ride." If you think about it, isn't that the way most people live their lives? You may have heard the saying, "By failing to plan, you plan to fail." I am sure you don't want that to be you. There is another saying, which says, "If you keep on doing what you've always done you'll keep on getting what you always got." The grammar may not be the best, but you no doubt get the idea.

You have probably heard about setting goals your entire life. Most likely you have set goals at different times in your life. Maybe you've achieved them and maybe you haven't. Very few people who have set goals have taken the time to write them down. I believe if you haven't taken the time to write them down you weren't totally committed to achieving them. There is truly something wonderful and extremely powerful that takes place just by the process of writing down your goals. I've heard it described as magical. Whatever you want to call it, I can assure you that it works.

IS THIS THE WAY YOU TRAVEL? "WE DON'T KNOW WHERE WE'RE GOING, BUT WELCOME ABOARD!"

You have already started the process of goal setting by completing the exercises thus far. We're now going to take it to another level. If you've never gone through a goal setting workshop before this will be an eye-opening experience for you—we'll have some fun, too. If you have you may be thinking, "I've done this already, I already know what my goals are," and you're ready to go to the next chapter. Resist the temptation to skip this part because we're most likely going to do it differently than what you experienced before. Besides, I guarantee you have either forgotten some of your goals or your goals have changed from what they were before. As we get older we begin to look at life differently, our priorities change, and the things we used to believe were important may not seem so anymore. I'll be honest with you, I used to hate goal setting workshops because I would get so focused on attaining the goals I had written down I forgot to enjoy my life. I also became extremely frustrated and even angry with myself when I didn't achieve the success I had scripted for myself—once again the wrong way to go about it. Because of my sales background I looked at goals the way I looked at sales quotas—something I would be punished for not attaining. I don't want you to look at this workshop that way. Look at the things you write down as desires, like your vacation itinerary. If you planned to see a certain site but couldn't fit it in did you punish yourself? I hope not, but some people do. Remember that your main goal in your life should be to enjoy every day of it. Come with me into the future for a moment. When you're lying on your deathbed and someone asks you if you have any regrets, do you think your answer will be "I wish I'd spent more time in the office?" Chances are your regrets will be more along the lines of family, relationships, love, spiritual growth, personal fulfillment, or giving more of yourself for the benefit of others.

The first thing you need to know about this workshop is that we'll be talking about several different types of goals. I believe the most important goals we should have are for self-improvement. By getting this far in this book you're probably not surprised by that are you? Jim Rohn is fond of saying, "It's not what you get out of life that counts, it's what you become." I like that a lot. If you think about it, though, you will get out of life the things you want by first becoming the person you want to be. Unlike "which came first, the chicken or the egg," there's no mystery here at all. If your expectation as to how you expect to get financial freedom is by winning the lottery—and I doubt you'd be still reading this book if that were you—you're apt to be sorely disappointed. I've got news for you, if you think that money will make you happy—it won't. Look at the famous and wealthy people in the entertainment and sports industries. How many of them are truly happy? Money will get you more of what you've already got. If you're normally sad now, you'll be miserably depressed when you get wealth unless you change the way you look at yourself and the world first. Read the Biographies of Howard Hughes, Marilyn Monroe, Jim Morrison, Janis Joplin, John Belushi, Richard Pryor, Kurt Cobain and others. You no doubt can name many more than this. Don't get me wrong, I've got nothing against money at all, in fact I like it. All I'm saying is that happiness has nothing to do with wealth. I've read many stories of people who have won the lottery who admit that they were much happier before they won. Now, if you have your life in order, have great relationships, and understand what really makes you happy, and then get financial freedom your life will get even better. Again, money gives you the freedom to be more of what you already are. In this workshop we will focus on several areas of your life that will help you achieve balance. The areas I'd like you to consider include:

1. Personal growth and development
2. Spiritual growth
3. Career goals
4. Money
5. Things
6. Relationships
7. Health and energy
8. Variety
9. Personal fulfillment
10. Giving unselfishly for the benefit of others

A SYNERGY OF PARTS
TO MAKE A COMPLETE PERSON

The illustration of the jigsaw puzzle can help you to think of your life as a mosaic made up of different parts. All of these parts fit together precisely to make you the complete person. If you take one or more of the pieces away the puzzle begins to fall apart. There is a synergy of these pieces that makes you more than the sum of the individual parts.

I believe that the happiest people have balance in their lives, which encompasses these ten areas. Keep in mind that money and things may go together somewhat, but they can also be completely separate. Although money can certainly buy things, it can also provide freedom to accomplish other goals as well. For some people money means influence, which for them can provide personal fulfillment. For others money can provide the means to give unselfishly for the benefit of others. Money may also be necessary to provide health and energy.

For the next five minutes I would like you to write down every idea that comes into your mind as to what you would like your life to provide. Allow yourself to dream big dreams. You are not a trained flea. The only limits your life has are those that you put on yourself.

The best approach to coming up with your true desires is what we call brainstorming. Brainstorming can be done in a group to initiate new and creative ideas. In a group setting there should never be judgments given on the value of ideas put forward while the session is ongoing. Judging the value of ideas during the process limits creativity. In this exercise you will brainstorm with yourself. You will want to write down every idea that comes into your mind without judging whether it is good or bad. In fact, you should abbreviate your thoughts—you'll be able to decipher it later—so that you can get the most ideas in the shortest amount of time. Remember that every time you try to appraise the negative value of a particular thought you allow some negative emotions to come into play. These negative thought processes—and the negative emotions attached to them—scare away the creative thought processes that are waiting within you to be released. Later you will go back and evaluate the true value of your thoughts as you prioritize them. But for now you will write down everything that comes into your mind no matter how trivial it may seem to you. Before we get into specific categories I'd like you to write down—without thinking about it—ten things you would do if you had unlimited courage.

1.
2.
3.
4.
5.
6.
7.
8.
9.
10.

Now, go back and pick the top five things you would most like to do if you had no fears, no doubts, and unlimited courage.

Now I would like you to go back and put a completion date next to each of your top five goals by when you will have accomplished it.

Now, write a paragraph for each of your top five goals—starting with number one—describing why you want to do this, what benefits will it bring to you and/or others, and most importantly how will it make you feel when you have done it?

1.

2.

3.

4.

5.

Now make an action plan for each one of your top five, beginning with the one with the earliest completion date. Make your action plan for goal number one start with some positive action today.

1.

2.

3.

4.

5.

Can you take your first action step right now? Remember that winners take action. You most likely appreciate that your enthusiasm and commitment to any goal fades as time passes. Take action right now while the commitment is freshest in your mind. Go ahead, I'll wait....

Did you take action on goal #1? If you did, congratulations, you are on your way.

Now, I'd like you to take the time to write down three goals for personal growth. After each goal you'll need to establish a time frame for accomplishing it whether it be something you can do immediately, in the next six months, one year, five years, whenever:

1.

2.

3.

Now, if you will, write down why you have set these goals for yourself. In other words, what will they do for you? What positive changes will be made in your life for others and for you by you reaching each of these goals in the time frame you have given it?

1.

2.

3

WHAT IS A TIMELINE?

Now, to fully gain leverage on your mind you will need to take yourself to the future. Make believe you're an old man or woman looking back on your life. Another way to think about this is this: If you could get in a time machine and transport yourself to the future what will it look like as a result of your having achieved each of these personal goals? In *Back to the Future, Star Trek* and shows like this, a timeline is a different future changed by some event in the past. Your present life is a result of all the events in your past. If you could take a time machine and go back in time and change certain events in your life your present would be greatly different wouldn't it? By changing an event in your past you would have begun a different timeline with a different future. This you can't do. You and I can do nothing about events in the past, but your destiny awaits you based on what you do in your life starting today. The past does not equal the future.

You're now in the future, reflecting back on your past. What was your life like as a result of achieving each of these goals? Make the visualizations (images) as real as you possibly can. If you can get to your place of solitude where you can really be alone make the pictures as vivid as they can be of what your life has been like. How satisfied and happy are you with yourself for realizing your dreams? Let yourself feel the feelings of joy and satisfaction. What are the pictures that you see? What are the colors? What sounds do you hear? What are the smells of your happy life? In *It's A Wonderful Life* George Bailey was able to see what the world would have been like if he had never been born and then was given another chance at his life. The people in George Bailey's world were greatly benefited by his having been in their lives. Have others been benefited by the new you? Let yourself see their happy faces. What does it feel like knowing how you've helped them?

Once you've mastered these positive visualizations I would like you to change the timeline. In this timeline you never made these changes—you're exactly the same person you are today without ever taking action towards the realization of your goals. Now you're looking back on your life, as it will be without these goals ever having been attained, as George Bailey saw when he never existed. Let yourself feel the disappointment—don't hold it back. What do you see now? What do you hear? What are the smells? Your mind needs to understand the price you will pay for not making the changes you have outlined for yourself.

Are you done? Is your mind totally committed now to your successful achievement of these very important goals? Good. Now you will need to write down a plan of action. What steps will you take beginning today to make your positive timeline a reality? Remember that all success begins with action. Your assignment for today is to complete a plan of action on how you will attain these personal self-improvement goals you have set for yourself. It's very important that you take your first positive action today. Do it while it's the freshest in your mind. Develop this as your personal philosophy or one of your self-beliefs: "I am a person who takes action now." Combining the visualizations, which you've already done, with action now, will make your dreams of your future come true.

Action plan steps: When started: When completed:
1.
2.
3.
4.
5.

What action will I do today to get myself started on the road to achieving my dreams?

Remembering that the happiest people have balance in their lives, what goals do you have in the following areas?

Spiritual growth

Money

Things

Relationships

Career goals

Health and energy

Variety

Giving unselfishly for the benefit of others

Just as you did before, you will need to go back now and put a completion date down for each of your top three goals in each area.

Then you will want to write at least three benefits you and/or others will receive from you accomplishing your goals.

Now you will want to make an action plan as to how you will accomplish these goals. Remember that taking action today creates a different timeline for your future than failing to take action.

If it makes sense to you to do so, go through your time machine visualization process with the two scenarios for each of the top three goals in each category. How will you feel about yourself and your life when you are much older reflecting back on your life for each timeline—reaching your goals, and not reaching them?

Congratulations. Just the act of writing down these important life goals makes many of them happen. There are many remarkable stories of people just like you who did nothing more than take the time to write down their goals. You have just done something that less than 1 out of 10 people on this planet ever do. You are an exceptional person. Remember that faith—positive thinking—directs your powerful mind to make your visualized future become your destiny. You're already halfway there. The more that you visualize the timeline of already having accomplished these goals the greater the reality of that future. Have fun, and I'll see you tomorrow.

Chapter Nineteen

Pain can be good for you—How to make your pain work for you!

Welcome to chapter nineteen. How did your goal setting go? Out of all the chapters in these pages the last two you have just read can have the most dramatic impact in the direction your life takes from this point on. Nothing else I've experienced has quite the effect as writing down ones goals and making an action plan for achieving them—assuming you follow through on your plan. If you took the time to thoroughly do your goal setting, congratulations! You have just done something that over 90% of the people in the world NEVER do. Are you now believing me when I say you are an exceptional person? Your clear visualizations of your new future will program your subconscious to follow through whether you're consciously aware of it or not. You are well on your way to reaching the future of your new timeline. You will want to review your written goals frequently to keep yourself headed in the direction you have chosen for your life. You're doing extremely well.

PAIN CAN EMPOWER YOU..

We know that everything we as human beings do is either to gain pleasure or avoid pain. As simplistic as this sounds it really is the fundamental motivation for all human behaviors. Of course the infinite variety of life's experiences can many times confuse what pain is and what pleasure is. An example of this is an athlete who is pushing himself or herself to the wall of personal effort in order to achieve a personal goal. I was watching the old ABC series Wide World of Sports a few years ago. In a Triathlon a female athlete pushed herself so hard to finish the race that she lost control of her bodily functions. In front of a worldwide audience she did something that would normally cause great embarrassment for almost anyone. And yet, after the race was over—which she finished crawling on her hands and knees—she took great pride in the fact she finished in spite of "hitting the wall" as they call it. For many people "embarrassment" is one of the greatest pains—something they would do almost anything to avoid. And yet, for this woman it wasn't embarrassment at all, but a source of pride. You now know that you have the ability to look at the pain in your life however you choose to. You can use your pain as a tool to empower you, or you can let it limit your joy, and your growth as a human being. The flea can't do this, but you can.

The expression "no pain, no gain" is almost a cliché in bodybuilding and many other physical endeavors. Pain, therefore, for people undergoing sports conditioning is looked at as a good thing—to a point of course. Marines, Navy Seals, Green Berets, and other top notch special military units look at the pain they must endure in training as a "badge of honor"—something to strive for. This is what we call re-framing—a term you are now familiar with.

I heard a story recently of a girl whose body did not have the ability to feel pain. This story opened my eyes and allowed me to look at pain in a different light. When you put your hand on a hot stove, what happens? The body's pain mechanism goes to work instantly alerting your brain that there is severe danger, and the pain causes a reflex action—no conscious thought necessary—causing you to remove your hand immediately. You may suffer a burn, because the reflex in some cases isn't quick enough to avert all damage, but think what would happen if your body had no pain mechanism. You might leave your hand on that stove until severely burned, or worse. Think what would happen if you felt no pain when you broke a bone, or if you fell down. How would you know a bone was even broken if you felt no pain? When you rub your eye, how do you know how hard to rub? For this little girl her lack of the normal pain mechanism was tragic. She looked as if she had been severely burned, or tortured in some way. Much of her body was deformed by physical abuse which she inflicted on herself simply because she couldn't tell the difference. For example, several of her fingers were stubs, which had literally been burned or broken away because her pain mechanism, which was supposed to protect her, didn't.

Pain is the body's natural alert mechanism

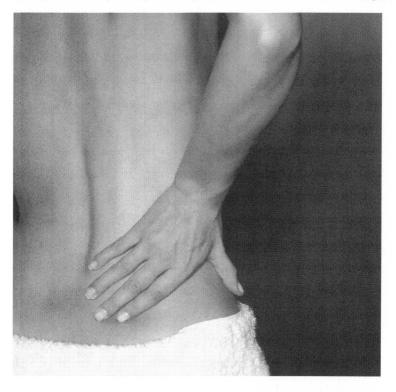

What can we learn from this? Clearly pain can teach us what we can do and what we can't do. In the case of your efforts to become all you can be, your pain can be a motivating force for positive change. As an adult who now understands that you have the power and the will to change your mental associations for your own empowerment, you can use the pain you've experienced in the past as a force for good. Just as your pain mechanism advantages your physical body, the pain mechanism of your life's experience can empower you in your efforts to become all you're capable of being. You already know how to do this. Hopefully by now you have developed the habit of asking yourself the right—empowering—questions to turn every negative situation into a positive one. Just as the body's pain mechanism protects you and empowers you, your being sensitive to negative— pain causing—events should trigger your mental mechanism to re- frame the event into a positive one. Initially you have to consciously make the effort to do this. Eventually it will become a habit where you no longer even think about it. Remember when you were first learning to drive? (If you don't drive perhaps you know someone who went through this). Every action was difficult, wasn't it? You didn't know how far to turn the wheel to make the car corner just the way you wanted it. You didn't know how hard to push the brakes to come to a controlled comfortable stop. Perhaps you were afraid to take your eye off the road even for a second to adjust the volume on the radio. But after you'd driven for awhile everything became automatic didn't it? If you've been driving for even a few months all the actions that were a struggle for you are now habits. Now you can talk on your cellular phone, tune the radio, put the turning signal on, safely stop the car and even chew gum all at the same time. You have habits whether you want them or not. The key to a successful, happy life is having the right ones. An old adage you would do well to memorize is "Sew a thought reap an action, sew an action reap a habit, sew a habit reap a destiny."

THOUGHTS ARE THINGS...

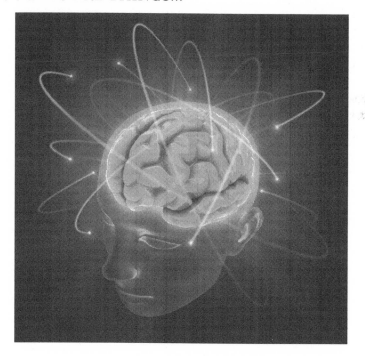

Thoughts are things, just as a table is a thing. Everything we do has some effect on something or someone. You know that you become whatever you think about on a regular basis. Your actions are a direct result of whatever you allow yourself to think about. If you think negative thoughts you will experience negative emotions. In all cases this results in a negative behavior that harms you and/or someone else. These are things that neither you nor I can change— they just are. A saying I really like is, "Some things are; whether you believe in them or not." If you don't believe in gravity that doesn't change the fact that it exists. Our thoughts have an impact on our lives and others around us whether we believe they do or not. You, therefore, in knowing this can use it to your advantage—taking positive control, or you can let your thoughts control you. There will be outcomes either way. They will either be outcomes you desire or ones you don't—the choice is yours?

Your assignment for today is to write down three situations in your life where pain—either physical or emotional—had a negative impact on you at least in the short term.

1.

2.

3.

Now, thinking back on your life, I would like you to write down what positive effects this has had for you. If this sounds strange to you—or even impossible at first—remember that your mind will always give you the right answer to the right question. Ask yourself what you learned from the painful experience. Did it make you grow somehow? Did it help someone else to grow? Are there people in your life today who have great meaning to you who would not have been there if this pain event had never happened? I can tell you from my own life that I have had many pain events—including the death of my father, a terrible disease, and changes in employment which I would have never asked to have happened. Even though at the time I wouldn't have believed it, each of these events has had positive effects on my life. What's the point? Simply this: Bad things are going to happen to you just as they happen to every person who has ever lived. This you can't change. What you can change, however, is how you look at these events. I know without even knowing you that you can think of people who you know personally who have seemingly had every benefit and still managed to be miserable. You also know others who have had every obstacle thrown in their path, but have somehow managed to live happy and beneficial lives. Life is what you make it. I challenge you to find a positive/positives from these three events that at the time seemed terrible to you. The biography in the next chapter will give you an example of what I'm talking about. See you tomorrow.

CHAPTER TWENTY

BIOGRAPHY

We've spent considerable time discussing positive attitudes, and not allowing negative thoughts and emotions in our daily lives. We've talked about focus and looking for the positive aspect in any given situation. That's easy to say when things are going well and some little problem pops up, but what about when something major hits us like a knock-out punch coming from nowhere? What about something so terrible that many would simply succumb to it and give up—What then?

Joan Bova had led the perfect life. In her own words: "It was like an Ozzie and Harriet family. Mom was a homemaker, and Dad owned his own service station and ran a fuel oil business. They both had great Christian values, and were always there for me. I was always involved in youth groups at our small Christian school, which was attached to our church. I loved to horseback ride, and was pretty much a tomboy—I just wanted to keep up with my brothers who were six and eight years older. As the only girl, I was spoiled rotten, and I loved every minute of it. It was just wonderful!"

After her family moved from Jacksonville when she was only two, she grew up in Orlando. Shortly after her twelfth birthday she noticed that her right wrist was hurting. She didn't think too much of it at first—she was a tomboy, after all, and she and her brothers were always roughhousing. A few days later, though, she noticed a similar feeling in her left wrist. Mom now started to be concerned as her little girl was also running a low-grade fever. The family had a hunch that it was Rheumatic Fever. She was checked into the hospital, and for the first time in her young life, she was away from her family over night. The tests confirmed that she had Juvenile Rheumatoid Arthritis. The disease is believed to be hereditary, although there was no history in the family that anyone knew about. "Soon," she recalls, "I began to feel "yucky." The effects of the disease spread rapidly. Within a month she could no longer run.

"I remember thinking how much I missed running," she says. "I could remember what it was like to run, but I just couldn't do it anymore." Now, many years later, she can no longer remember what it felt like.

Joan's family owned two horses and often went to rodeos, and her very favorite thing to do was horseback riding. Before long, Joan began experiencing tremendous pain in her hips every time she rode. Within a couple months after her diagnosis she was never to ride again. Soon, even walking became very painful.

Besides the arthritis, there was much going on in the life of this young girl. As she was now going into the seventh grade, she no longer would go to the little private Christian school attached to her church. She would now attend a much larger school with kids she had never known—kids who could run and play. John F. Kennedy was President, and he had recently instituted a major emphasis on physical education. It was mandatory for all students. Joan remembers trying to play volleyball, but when the ball came to her and she hit it, her wrist turned completely backwards. The pain was excruciating, but she refused to cry. Finally, she had to summon the courage to tell the teacher and the principal that she just couldn't play the games the other kids could. She was humiliated and hurt that she could only sit and watch the other kids play. Never a big girl, she began to drop weight rapidly. Now resembling a stick, her joints got stiffer and stiffer.

The other kids stared at her began to stare at her. One day another girl asked her directly, "What is wrong with you?"

"I'll tell you later," Joan said, not knowing what else to say. Every day for a week the girl would ask her and she'd answer, "I'll tell you later." Eventually, the girl's persistence forced an explanation.

"I just felt like a big pimple!" Joan now says, reflecting back on those days. Adults, in particular bothered her. "I remember the principal watching me as I walked past him, and I heard him say to himself, 'What a shame; tsk, tsk, tsk.' It made me so very angry, as I felt adults should know better. I felt no shame. I am the way I am, and there's nothing I can do about it. What is there to be ashamed of?"

Every Friday Mom and Joan went to the hairdresser together and then the grocery store. Walking from the hairdresser, down Orange Ave. in Orlando, her hips were really hurting her. A woman who looked a little older than her mother approached them and began to stare at her, gawking at her, as she looked her up and down. Joan glared back angrily. Later that night she couldn't get the woman's reaction to her and her own response out of her mind. Along with her humiliation and anger, she felt guilty, as she'd been trained to respect her elders. She realized, as she lay awake in bed that people were going to stare at her for the rest of her life. A plan formed in her mind that she's never broken. No one would ever make her feel that way again. Whenever someone would stare at her from that day forward she would look him or her in the eye and give them the biggest smile she could muster. "You know what?" she says, "It works every time. They smile right back!"

Joan now felt in control—the situation no longer controlled her. By the time she was fifteen she was in need of daily physical therapy as her joints were freezing up. Crutches were now a necessity—walking extremely difficult. The cost of the therapy was increasingly burdensome for her parents. Her doctor recommended the Harry Anna Crippled Children's Hospital. She still remembers her outrage at the sign when they drove to check it out that first day. "Crippled" was not a term she could relate to. Her Dad had taught her that she could do anything in her life if she wanted it badly enough. He'd say, "You're okay, honey." And she believed him. Reluctantly she went inside—It was charming! Harry and Anna Miller had donated this lovely 3-story stucco home—which had for awhile been used as a hotel—to the Elks, for children with disabilities. People in those days were not as sensitive to the terminology we use today, hence the name "Crippled Children's Hospital," though it was really more like a home.

Even though the only night she had ever been away from her family was that one terrible day in the hospital—when she cried all night long, —she decided to stay. It was a decision that changed her life. A whole New World opened for her. She wasn't the "odd-kid" anymore, as all these kids—mostly teenagers around her own age—had severe disabilities. She was now among her own kind. Her natural leadership abilities began to blossom. The time period—the 60's—worked for her there as well. There was a girls' ward; and a boys' ward. There were all-night slumber parties, and dates to the movies. The leaders of the hospital went out of their way to make things normal and wonderful. Josie Cadwell, The Director of Nurses, would remind them often, "You are normal, healthy teen-agers," and the kids believed her.

Her unique creative talents, leadership, and communication skills were soon utilized in a variety of ways. Once a year there was a big Elks convention and the kids were a part of the program. Joan helped to coordinate the talent show, and her own comedy routine was a big hit. Before long she was a featured speaker on behalf of the Harry Anna in public relations events with the local media. The next four years flew by. They were good times.

Joan's difficulties had just begun. At nineteen she began to experience double vision; Her speech began to slur, and the more she talked, the worse it became. For someone who loved to talk as much as Joan, it was as if Murphy's Law was playing its ultimate cruel joke. Soon, she had difficulty swallowing. A neurologist discovered that she had Myasthenia Gravis, the disease that Aristotle Onassis—Jackie Kennedy's husband—had developed late in his life. Her nerves were sending messages to the muscles, but the muscles couldn't interpret the messages. Now, unable even to support her head, she was confined to bed for over a year. The doctors prescribed a medication but it was almost impossible for her to even swallow the pills. Eventually, her condition improved somewhat, but because she had been confined to bed for so long, and unable to move her joints, she now used a wheelchair.

Her twenties were spent just trying to remain alive. She was five feet tall, and weighed only 85 lbs.— she had grown only one more inch since she was twelve. After going into respiratory distress—only being saved by a last effort tracheotomy—she was in the hospital for two months. A Neurologist, Dr. Victor Robert—her savior, she now calls him—had just arrived in Orlando from New York. He determined that her medication was insufficient and he recommended the removal of her thymus gland. The thymus is key to fighting infection in young people, but is supposed to shrink as we get older. Joan's had never shrunk, causing antibodies to flood into her system to fight an infection, which she didn't have. When she left Orlando Regional Medical Center she was taking 22 pills per day. Within 2 months she was down to only 8. Her health improved rapidly.

Joan is now 50 years old. She is the Director for Community Relations for the Center for Independent Living in Winter Park, Fl. Her warmth and charm—combined with her passion for living—are perfectly suited for her role in raising awareness of the wonderful work done by this private, not-for-profit organization. CIL—totally funded by private donations, some Federal grants, some State and County funds, and the United Way—provides a variety of services at no charge to those who fall under the ADA (Americans with Disabilities Act)—currently 54 million people in the United States. CIL provides:

  a) Information and referral (where to go for help).
  b) Skills training
  c) Peer support (51+% of directors and staff must have disabilities)
  d) Advocacy (lobbying efforts and PR on behalf of the disabled.

Maybe most importantly of all, the CIL teaches the disabled how to advocate for themselves. The ADA definition of a disabled person is anyone with a physical or mental impairment that substantially limits one or more major life activities—such as hearing, walking, seeing, speaking, working, taking care of oneself, learning, or breathing. CIL helps to arrange for independent living for those who in former years would have been forced into institutions.

Joan has had many jobs in her 17-year career at CIL, the first one doing just that—helping to locate living facilities for those needing it.

In addition to her job, Joan has been an active volunteer for many years. For the last eight years she has traveled extensively as the head of Disabilities Ministries in the southern states. She gives freely of her time and talents in an effort to raise public awareness on behalf of those with disabilities. She also educates on how to build churches with the needs of the disabled in mind. Never forgetting her own experiences, she teaches the non-disabled how to act towards those they perceive as different from themselves.

Joan and her husband of 17 years accepted foster children into their home for 9 years, finally adopting two biological sisters almost four years ago. Angela (17) and Kristina (16) have been theirs now since August 1996. Joan met her husband, a freelance writer, through Church, shortly after successful knee replacement surgery for both legs in 1979—a surgery, which allowed her to stand for the first time in ten years. Something the vast majority of us take for granted— the ability to stand—was for her another miracle, for she could now transfer herself from her wheelchair into a car or into her bath, or bed. She was liberated and free.

Joan Bova is an inspiration to everyone who knows her—she certainly is to me. Her enthusiasm for life and her sincere interest in others is remarkable. She wants to leave the world a better place for those who come after her. The legacy she strives for every day of her life is for the non-disabled to treat the disabled like "normal" people. After all, she says, "We're just people."

Maybe she's right, but after getting to know Joan, I would have to say that she, for one, is much more than that.

(Update as of 1/12/09)- Joan left CIL in 2000 and worked for Central Florida Legal Services teaching disabled persons about fair housing laws. In 2002 she underwent serious surgery requiring complete reconstruction of her cervical spine. For the last 10 years she has directed the Disabilities Ministries Program for nine southern states. She continues to use her unique teaching abilities for the benefit of others.

Your assignment for today:

What about Joan's life experience can I apply in my own life?

What circumstances or events in my life have been negative for me? (Name at least three)

How can I reframe these experiences and find something positive from them.?

If these events happened a long time ago, what positives resulted from them? (This may be difficult, but try really hard to come up with some).

If these events were more recent, what can you do to turn them into something positive for your future. No matter what has happened to you or will happen there are no benefits in letting the perception of the event negatively impact your life. Remember, every event in your life can be perceived by you as positive or negative. Your perception is your reality. Your perceptions determine what you do as a result of the event, whether you let them destroy you, or cause negative results to you and those around you, or whether you use them to benefit you and those you care about.

Chapter Twenty-one

Mind and Body

M ost of what we have dealt with in this book has to do with conquering the challenges of your mind. In fact, in our opening chapter we talked about winning the war in the battlefield of your mind. It's important for you to understand, though, that it is impossible to separate the control and performance of your mind and thoughts from the physical part of you. Not only do your thought processes affect your physiology, but the opposite is true as well. You can greatly affect your thought processes, your attitude about yourself, and the way you feel at any given moment by your physiology.

Happy or sad?

They are truly inseparable. When I first started in sales it was constantly stressed that prospects were impressed by your enthusiasm for your product or service. I found it interesting at the initiation of my sales career that you were supposed to be sold on your product in order to sell it effectively. An acronym was used in training new sales people—enthusiasm. Enthusiasm is a state of mind, isn't it? We were taught that enthus*iasm* could be defined as the last four letters—IASM. **I Am Sold Myself.** Certainly it is true that if you are truly sold on something you naturally will be enthusiastic when you talk about it, wouldn't you agree? This involves the thought process and your belief system, which we have spent considerable time on thus far. But if you've ever sold anything for very long you know that sooner or later your enthusiasm wanes somewhat. This doesn't necessarily mean that you no longer believe in the value of your product or service, but it is human nature to be less excited about things that are no longer new to us. That is why we were also taught that in order to be enthusiastic we should *act* enthusiastic. Your physiology—the physical process of acting enthusiastic—has a powerful impact on your thought processes. The mind and the body are truly inseparable. If you think about the way someone looks when they are depressed what picture comes to your mind? Don't you think about someone whose shoulders are slumped forward, who's most likely looking downward? Don't you have an image in your mind of someone whose facial muscles are rather slack, and whose breathing is rather shallow?

It's interesting that you can change the way you feel just by the way you stand, by the way you breathe, by the focus of your eyes and where you are looking, by the way you move your facial muscles. Now, form an image in your mind of someone who is excited about something. What do they look like? Are they animated in their facial features? Are they standing erect? Are their gestures more dramatic? Do their eyes have a different focus and a sparkle that the depressed person didn't have? It is a fact that you can change the way you feel just by the way you act. You can make yourself enthusiastic about something by acting like you are. So, I ask you, which comes first, the chicken or the egg? Do you act excited about something because your mind tells you that you are? —Or do you feel excited about something because your body acts like it is? Both are true, aren't they? There really is no wrong or right answer here.

HOW ABOUT THIS ONE?

We have discussed that most of us would much rather feel happy than sad. We would rather be excited and enthused than depressed and unhappy. We've talked about Peter Pan and your "happy thoughts." You know that you can take yourself to a happy place whenever you want to. These are purely mental processes. I would like to tell you now that if you want your mind to function at its best and give you the control and thoughts that most likely are some of your goals you will need to add some physical exercise to your daily life. If the thought of exercise scares you, I'm sorry. Remember that some things are true whether we want them to be or not. This isn't something I created—it's a truism of life. Physical exercise releases endorphins into the bloodstream, which helps create a sense of well being. I have noticed with myself that no matter how well I do with

153

asking myself the right questions, and only allowing positive thoughts in my mind I have some difficulty feeling good about myself and my world if I don't exercise regularly. This effect is well documented. I am not telling you anything you haven't heard before when I say that regular exercise is extremely beneficial for you. Don't misunderstand me, I'm not saying that if you're not used to regular exercise you should go out and run a marathon, or even start jogging. Meet with your doctor and get on a regular exercise program that starts off slowly and progresses to at least 20 minutes of continuous exercise at least three times per week. If you can add resistance training to this on alternate days, so much the better. Resistance training increases lean muscle mass, increases strength and endurance, raises the body's metabolism, and can have dramatic affects on your physical appearance. All these things can greatly add to your positive feelings about yourself and the world around you. Find a type of exercise you truly enjoy. Walking, riding a bicycle, playing tennis or basketball, swimming; all of these are excellent. How about playing racquetball? Please don't look at this as drudgery. Remember to ask yourself the right questions every day. Ask yourself, "What exercise can I do today that I will enjoy, that will make me feel good about myself and help me to be healthier?" Many have had success increasing their exercise by getting in the habit of taking the stairs instead of riding the elevator.

FIND SOMETHING YOU ENJOY..

Can you park further away from the office, grocery store, or whatever and walk further? Instead of driving to the corner store for a gallon of milk and the newspaper, can you take a brisk walk or ride your bicycle? If you enjoy gardening, can you garden intensely for at least twenty minutes for at least three times per week? If this is too difficult for you initially, can you start doing ten minutes several times a day? You have to start somewhere. How about rollerblading, skiing, or ice-skating? I would be greatly surprised if you don't agree that your mental powers and your sense of self-worth increase when you start regularly exercising. Remember to have fun doing it— that's key. If exercise has never been fun for you find someone to do it with whose company you enjoy. The only caution that I have for you here is that when you depend on someone else to exercise with you what happens when they can't? This is something you need for your physical health, your mental health, and your own sense of well being. Don't short-change yourself here. Join a health club if you must. Get a personal trainer if that will help you. Can you buy some interesting exercise DVD's to motivate you at home? If you are thinking you're too old I've got news for you. My Mom is 85 years old with bad arthritis and she briskly walks for 30 to 45 minutes every day. If you live in an area where the climate isn't conducive to this—sorry, my Mom lives in Buffalo, NY. When she can't walk outside because it's too cold or snowy she walks around inside the house—around and around from room to room. I'm not telling you to take a brisk walk today for 30 minutes if you get winded just going to the mailbox, but you have to start somewhere. Start easy and set incremental improvements for yourself until you're doing at least 30 minutes a day. There really is no excuse unless you're a quadriplegic and even then there are exercises you can do which will help you. I've heard Christopher Reeves give several talks at different seminars and in spite of his terrible accident he maintained a positive attitude by believing that his condition was only temporary. He also exercised regularly within the constraints of his physical condition. If he could do it, so can you. Develop the discipline to do this and I guarantee you that you'll be glad you did.

TENNIS ANYONE?

If one of the reasons you bought this book was because you desire to lose weight and have always had trouble in this area, maybe exercise is the element you have been missing. Most of the people I've known in my life who have a weight problem live relatively sedentary lives. Just as in all generalizations, this isn't always true, but for many it is. Losing weight is a relatively simple formula. Once again, I said simple, not easy. For many, controlling their weight is one of life's biggest challenges. The basics are taking in fewer calories than your body burns. You know this already don't you? By increasing your exercise level you're already half way there. Maybe you have tried eating low-fat or fat free foods and that hasn't worked. Most of those foods are loaded with extra sugar to give them a better taste. Sugar quickly turns to fat if the body doesn't use all the calories. What's worse is that sugar throws the blood sugar level higher causing you to get hungry again even quicker, which causes you to eat even more.

Also, the more sweet foods you eat the more your taste buds become insensitive to foods with lower levels of sugar which causes you to crave more sweets. What's the answer? You need to train your taste buds to enjoy the tastes of real natural foods such as vegetables, fruits, whole-grains (unprocessed). The only way I've found to do this is by severely limiting any processed sugars from my diet. If you must sweeten things use honey, but try to reduce your intake of sugar. Instead of eating processed low-fat foods you need to reduce your consumption of fatty meats and oils. Most experts will tell you that 30% or less of your total calories should be from fat. You can't make up for eating fatty foods by eating more calories from processed low or no fat foods, though. It just doesn't work that way. Every effective weight loss program I've seen also stresses drinking at least eight glasses of water each day. The water gives you a sense of fullness and also helps to raise your metabolism. Just as much of what you've read in these pages is a matter of perspective, proper diet and health definitely is. For many, just the word diet sounds like severe punishment—Who wants to *die*-et? Instead you need to get a different outlook on the whole process. It's not a temporary painful effort with an ending once you reach your weight-loss goal; it's a way of life. And it doesn't have to be painful. You know by now that for many any change is painful to some degree—Remember fear of change? Change occurs when the pain of the present is greater than the pain of change. To be successful in getting the personal appearance and health you desire your mind needs to understand that the pain of change really isn't that painful at all. Find a way to make it enjoyable. Remember that the quality of your life depends to a great extent on the quality of the questions you ask yourself each day. How about asking yourself, "How can I eat more healthy today and have fun doing it?" By combining proper eating habits with regular exercise and looking at the process as a life goal you can actually enjoy the process. Your visualization techniques can also help your mind understand that the pleasure of the future "new you" is much greater than the pain of changing the way you look at food and exercise. Take the new you into the future with your time machine. Compare the "old you" as you drag that future with you five, ten, fifteen years ahead. Another neat idea that works is cutting your head off of one of your pictures and taping it on the body you want to have. Put that picture on your refrigerator next to a current picture of yourself in a skimpy bathing suit. Or, if you're pretty good with a computer—or have a friend who is—you can digitally put your head on any body you want. Put the "new you" on your desktop on your PC. It never hurts to remind yourself often of your personal goals. Remember that you owe it to yourself and those around you to be the happiest with yourself that you can be. The more you like yourself the better everything else in your life becomes. As we've said already, you can do nothing of the past—the you of yesterday is yesterday. Forgive yourself for yesterday's failures and get on the right track for the future you desire. Today begins a new time-line for you. Which time-line do you want to be your future? Start the new you today. You'll be glad you did. The following is a list of foods you should try to avoid at all costs. If these are your absolute favorites, once again I'm sorry. But, if you're really committed to being the person you desire, you will have to make some changes. Remember that if you keep on doing what you've always done, you'll keep on getting what you always got—it's just a fact.

1. Potato chips
2. Candy
3. Soda pop
4. Most snack foods (high in salt and fat content—almost no fiber)
5. Fatty foods
6. Any food higher than 30% fat content (read the label)

So many books have been written on dieting and weight control that I can't begin to count them. There are numerous support groups for weight loss and dozens of commercial enterprises to help you lose weight. Maybe you've tried several of them. I certainly am not intending this chapter to be the definitive word on diet and health, but I can assure you that the basics you have just read agree with almost all the experts on the subject. Most fad diets are just that—fads. The only real positive you're likely to get out of them is that they will break your normal eating pattern, but to get long-term results you will need to get a different outlook on food and exercise. One of the problems we have in the US is that most restaurants provide portions that most of us can't eat and maintain an optimum weight unless our exercise level and metabolism is much higher than average. My wife and I normally will share a portion designed for one person and that works well. Many of our friends do the same thing. If you eat at fast food restaurants often you have even a worse challenge. Most of the combo meals that are so common now are extremely high in fat grams, low in fiber, and high in overall calories. Combine this with a large soda and you've got a recipe to overweight for sure.

Your assignment for today is this:

1. Make a list of five ways you can get more exercise every day. Ask yourself what exercise you can do that you'll have fun doing.

2. Make a list of the foods that you eat regularly that violate the rules you've just read.

3. Go through your visualizations with your time machine, taking yourself five years into the future, then ten years, then fifteen years, then twenty. Go through one series without making the changes we've outlined, and then go through another making today the beginning of a new timeline for your future.

4. Do the picture process described above. Put your head on the body you want and put that picture next to a recent picture of yourself wearing a skimpy bathing suit. Put these on your refrigerator and digitally on your computer desktop if you have one.

5. Make as detailed a list as you can of why you need to lose weight and increase your exercise. What will these things do to the way you feel? What other positive changes do you expect to happen in your life by making these changes? Write down at least ten positives that you will gain if you do and at least ten negatives that will happen if you don't.

6. Write down five things that you will start to do today to change your timeline for your desired future.

7. Start doing them today.

CHAPTER TWENTY-TWO

HOW TO BE MORE CREATIVE

A re you a creative person? If you answered yes, good—we'll explore that more in this chapter. If your answer was no, why do you answer that way? Is it because you've never done anything you would consider creative? I would guess that if we had videotape of your entire life that we could review from your childhood on we would find some examples that would prove you wrong. I believe—and there is much research to support this—that everyone is creative. There are some things I would like you to consider for a moment. Is there anyone else in the Universe exactly like you? Your experiences are totally unique, aren't they? Whether you believe that you were created by God, or that you are totally a magnificent accident of nature, the conclusion is inescapable. You are the only being on this planet—the entire Universe—with your experiences, your genetic material, and the interaction of those elements that makes you, you. Your thoughts are unique to you and you alone. The only difference between those who are revered as creative and those who aren't is that the creative ones believe they are and act on those beliefs.

DA VINCI WASN'T JUST A PAINTER......

Have you ever seen a commercial for a new product, or seen something on the store shelves for the first time and said to yourself, "I thought of that years ago?" Many people have had this experience, I know I have. The logical question, then, is who was the creative one? —You or the manufacturer? The only difference between you and the person/persons who brought the product to market was that they acted on their—or someone else's—inspiration, and you didn't. You may have dismissed your creativity because you simply couldn't believe that you came up with an original idea. Or, maybe you thought it was a good idea but you neglected to follow through on it. Often the only difference between creative and non-creative people is action. Action normally follows belief. If you believe that your ideas are truly creative and original most likely you will take action on them.

WHAT IF EDISON HAD KEPT THE
ELECTRIC LIGHT BULB A SECRET?

You may find it interesting to know that when Thomas Edison— the founder of GE—was finally successful in inventing the electric light bulb after failing nearly 10,000 times, most scientists and people of his day thought it was a silly idea. They were perfectly content lighting their way through life with oil burning lamps—that's the way it had been done for generations. Suppose he had kept it in his basement and not told anyone because he was afraid he'd be made fun of. Wilbur and Orville Wright's own father—Bishop Milton Wright—publicly stated that flight was meant only for angels and that the airplane would never "take off." Alexander Graham Bell was ridiculed for his pursuit of the invention of the telephone.

Just an eccentric artist's dream?

Leonardo da Vinci, who died in 1519, drew accurate pictures of flying machines centuries before they were invented and people scoffed, thinking him only an eccentric artist. Many today believe that if he had the right materials available to him he would have built a working model over 300 years before the Wright brothers. Creativity requires action, which in most cases requires overcoming fear of rejection, fear of failure, or fear of embarrassment.

By following the exercises we have set up for you thus far you have done much to position yourself for allowing your natural creativity to blossom forth. Negative thoughts and the negative emotions that always result from them stifle creativity. It is doubtful you'll be creative when you are angry. Some might argue though that artists do their best work when they are depressed. Although in some cases that might be the case I would think that their artistic efforts were a type of therapy for them. In that sense they were trying to overcome their negative emotions by taking some form of positive action. I know that when I was in my late teens and early twenties the only time I felt like writing was when I was depressed. I could have argued at that time in my life that my creativity came from negative feelings. Now, however, I don't believe that was true. When I was happy I felt I had better things to do than to sit in my room and write. In retrospect I can assure you that my writing was a form of therapy for me. At this time in my life I can tell you that I am my most creative and inspired when my mind is at peace. Anxiety and stress are definitely counterproductive to creativity.

It could be argued that most true creativity streams from the subconscious mind. Many writers will tell you that when they are at their best the words seem to come from nowhere. It's almost as if their fingers take on a life of their own and the words and thoughts appear on the word processor or on the paper. Some call this inspiration. Brian Tracey calls it the Superconscious Mind. Some call it Magic. In an earlier chapter we discussed that your subconscious stores the sum-total of your life's experiences. Since your inspiration in most cases comes from your experience it makes sense that creativity starts at the subconscious level. In Gary Fellers book *Creativity For Leaders* he talks of present mindedness. This harmonizes well with what we have discussed thus far in eliminating guilt, anger, anxiety, and fear from your life. Much of your success in doing this has to do with forgiveness of your past. Forgiving yourself, forgiving others, and asking yourself the right questions every day on how to become the person you want to be while having fun doing it. We have spent much time discussing that we need to find enjoyment in every aspect of our lives. Although we have specific goals for our future we need to remember that it is the present we are always living in. It is always the present where we will find our joy. If you don't believe this, think with me here. The goals you have set for yourself you have set because you believe you will get benefits from them when they are realized. Will you be in the future or the present when that happens? Although from your perspective of today that will be your future, when you get there it will be your present. By completely letting the past be the past and focusing on the moment your creativity will be at its best. Fellers lists *Twelve Steps To Creativity*. It's interesting to note that most of these steps have to do with eliminating the negative thoughts and emotions from our lives. Belief that your subconscious will give you the creativity you seek is germane to everything in this book, isn't it?   Belief, faith, and positive thinking are essentially all the same thing.

DON'T LET THE NAYSAYERS GET YOU DOWN!

The next step to maximizing your creativity is to keep a journal by your bed and at your office. Also have something with you at all times to either write them down or tape record your ideas when they come. Now that you believe in your creativity you will need to understand that inspiration can come at the times you least expect it. Possibly in the past you ignored these inspirations completely. Or, maybe you recognized them but because of your lack of belief in yourself you dismissed them. It is critical that you record them as soon as they come. If they come in a dream, tell your subconscious to wake you up so that you can write them down while they're fresh in your mind. Or, you can train your subconscious to remember your dreams so that you can write them down when you wake up.

Your creativity will also be enhanced if you are living the life you want to live as opposed to living the life others have thrust upon you. In our chapter on Career Planning we devoted much time to finding the one thing in your life that you would do for free. It would be advisable for you now to review that information. Remember *City Slickers*? The Billy Crystal character had to find his "one thing." True inspiration is much more likely when you are pursuing your life's dreams. The reasons should be clear to you by now, if they weren't before. Positive thoughts and emotions are a part of love. Your mind's true potential is opened up fully when the layers of negative thoughts are erased. When you truly love what you're doing your stress level is reduced, you're not anxious, you have no doubts, and consequently no fear. Your mind freely gives you the ways to make it happen for the benefit of others and yourself while you thoroughly enjoy the process. Isn't that the way you want to live?

Your assignment for today is to write down five ways that you can maximize the creativity that resides within you. Have you ever wanted to play an instrument, write a song, write poetry or a book? Are there better ways you have thought of at one time or another to do your job, make your home more attractive and livable, or help others to get greater joy in their lives? Let your mind run free—don't be afraid to dream. Take action on these five steps beginning today. Have fun, and I'll see you tomorrow.

1.
2.
3.
4.
5.

Chapter Twenty-three

Relationships

We've spent considerable time in the pages of this book talking about success. For most people we know that success means financial prosperity. Hopefully you agree that money—in and of itself—will not, and cannot make you happy. Many of the world's wealthiest individuals have made terrible messes of their lives. Many have involved themselves in destructive addictive behaviors; some have even killed themselves. Ernest Hemingway is someone I've been reading about recently who had everything anyone could want—you would think—and yet he committed suicide at age 61. Considered to be one of the greatest authors of all time, his life was full of adventure, creativity, and wealth that most could only dream of. And yet he was married four times and never seemed to find happiness. Howard Hughes is another historical example of great creativity, tremendous wealth and adventure, and yet he died a miserable recluse. Why? Of course, much of happiness comes from how we look at our lives and the world around us—This we know. But for most people the difference between joy and sadness can be summed up in two words: Meaningful relationships.

Where is your "Acres of Diamonds?"

If we are surrounded by people who we love and who love us in return, chances are we will feel pretty good about life. Of course, if our major focus is on gaining material wealth and we ignore the meaningful relationships we have developed that is a tragic mistake. Not only will we most likely ruin the relationships we have, but also when we get the wealth we'll realize that isn't where life's joy really comes from. By then it may be too late. This is sad, isn't it? You, no doubt, can think of many examples of people who fit these patterns. Can you name any Hollywood stars who have gone through marriage after marriage, drug addiction, alcoholism, stints at the Betty Ford Clinic, or other rehab programs? Or, how about people who have spent hundreds of thousands of dollars in psychotherapy trying to find some real meaning in their lives? My wife reminded me that one of the most cherished movies of all time deals with this very issue. The Wizard of Oz is the story of a young girl—Dorothy—who spends her days fantasizing about what life would be like over the rainbow. I'm sure you know the story—maybe better than I do. After her great adventure in the twister, in Munchkin Land, the Land of Oz, meeting Scarecrow, Tinman, and Cowardly Lion, when she wakes up she realizes that everything she ever wanted was right there all along. Remember how she kept repeating "There's no place like home."

You have probably seen the commercials on TV where someone gets extremely wealthy by sheer accident. One shows a man who trips over a shiny rock in his yard that turns out to be a huge gold nugget. Another shows a person who buys an antique picture frame at a yard sale and finds an original painting worth millions of dollars. The claim is that these stories are true. Another true story is one I first heard many years ago and I've heard it told in a number of ways since then. You may have heard it referred to as "Acres of Diamonds." The story first appeared in an essay around 1900. It's a true story of an African farmer who heard stories of diamond mines in other parts of Africa. He'd always dreamed of being wealthy, so he sold his farm and set out to find his fortune. He spent all the money from the sale of his farm searching all over the grand continent until finally broke and discouraged he walked into the sea and drowned himself. Meanwhile, the new owner of the farm discovered some unusual looking stones while working the farm. He took them into town and you guessed it—they were diamonds. It turned out that the entire farm was literally one huge diamond mine—one of the richest ever discovered. You may wonder—, as did I when I first heard it— why the farmer never noticed the diamonds on his own farm. The most likely answer is that we tend to take for granted that which we already have. The grass on the other side of the fence always looks greener than our own. We have spent considerable time in these pages discussing the filter of our own beliefs and how we perceive the world around us based on how we perceive ourselves. We have also discussed how people who don't like and love themselves have great difficulty liking and loving others. This is why negative thoughts and emotions are so destructive to others and to us. It is widely known that a high percentage of abusive parents were themselves abused when they were young.

When I started my own pursuit in the understanding of human behavior this was a puzzle I had great difficulty with. Why would someone who already knows what terrible suffering child abuse can bring do the same thing to his or her own children? I thought that a child who had undergone this would naturally do almost anything to make sure that his or her children wouldn't suffer the same fate. The logic of my earlier thoughts makes sense until you realize that almost nobody sets out to torment their children. In a way they can't help themselves. This is not to make an excuse for anyone's behavior by pointing to his or her childhood. Hopefully it is clear to you by now that I believe we are all responsible for own behavior, and the results of that behavior. What I am saying is that because of the abuse the person feels unworthy of love and as a result can't find a way to truly love others. It's an interesting phenomenon of human psychology that most of us clearly see the glaring weaknesses in those we are closest to which we subconsciously feel about ourselves. The fear, anger, and other negative emotions we harbor will always find an outlet—many times at the expense of those we would most like to protect from them. This is why it is so important that we forgive ourselves for our past mistakes, forgive everyone who has ever hurt us—either emotionally or physically—and develop the habits to bring the right—positive—thoughts into our minds on a regular basis. Once you have done this you may come to realize that your "Acres of Diamonds" are right in your own back yard.

Hopefully you agree that without meaningful relationships life has little joy no matter how much or little we may have in the way of material things. There has been much written about Relationship Building. In my sales career I have taken courses too numerous to name on how to develop relationships. I have read more books than I can even count. Of course, many of these were how to develop trust and confidence in business relationships. Most of them focus on "gaining rapport." In other words, how do you get someone to like you enough right away so that you can take the relationship further? Naturally you need rapport. Every course I have taken starts with the premise that people are naturally attracted to people they feel are like them. I know you've heard for years that "opposites attract." I'm sure you can name several examples of couples who have very different personalities. One is outgoing, the other shy. One has a dominant personality, the other somewhat docile. This may be true in romance—though not necessarily. But, generally in life, people are instantly attracted to others who they feel are like them. Relationship Building is a science unto itself. I've been to many workshops lasting several days on this subject. Different theories abound, but all of them say that there are four basic personality types. Understanding what yours is, and learning to recognize the characteristics of anyone else's is the key to gaining instant rapport. I will give you the basics in this chapter. You must understand that to become an expert on this you will need to devote much time and effort. After being in sales for 30 years and training hundreds of others in how to develop these skills I am still not successful 100% of the time in building instant rapport. Regardless of what some other trainers may say they're not always successful either. But, I can promise you that if you devote your energy to this you will see positive results, and you'll get better at it the more you practice. Like everything else in life—and everything we've discussed in this book—you'll want to develop the right habits so that it becomes automatic for you.

Some areas where good communication and rapport skills can reduce tension and improve relationship are:
1. Husband/wife
2. Parent/child
3. Sibling to sibling
4. Teacher/student
5. Supervisor/subordinate
6. Employee to employee
7. Peer to peer
8. Business negotiations
9. Sales calls

Think of how many more positive emotions you could experience if you were able to gain instant rapport with anyone. Have you ever wondered why some people just rub you the wrong way? Have you ever had the experience of not being able to get along with someone no matter how hard you tried? Or, wondered why your actions toward that person were always somehow misunderstood and misinterpreted? On the other hand, have you ever met someone where you felt an instant bond, as if you already knew the person for your entire life? Have you ever wondered why?

I've identified over one dozen models for behavioral styles, all with four categories. The earliest record made by astrologers discussed the positions of the heavens and 12 signs. Included were four basic groupings: earth, air, fire, and water. These are still used by some observers of behavioral styles today. Socrates discussed the four categories of blood, phlegm, black bile, and yellow bile. These were later expanded to give clarity and understanding as follows:

Sanguine-hopeful or confident
Phlegmatic-not easily agitated

Melancholy-easily dejected and gloomy

Choleric-bitter temper

In 1923, Dr. Carl Jung theorized that there are four Psychological Types. These are:

Intuitor - Values discovery, theory, and ideology. Focuses on ideas and concepts.

Feeler - Values family, friendship, and loyalty. Focuses on people and relationships

Thinker - Values ethics, and being right. Focuses on facts and analysis

Sensor - Values action, winning, and results. Focuses on action and results.

Allesandro and Associates describes the four personality types as follows:

Dominant Director

Interacting Socializer

Steady Relater

Cautious Thinker

Dr. John Geyer of Carlson Learning Company, Minneapolis, MN developed the Personal Profile System. He discusses four personality patterns, which include:

Dominance

Influence

Steadiness

Compliance

These four styles have observable patterns of behavior and they measure success in different ways:

1.Success measured by results

2.Success measured by acknowledgment and praise

3.Success measured by sharing and trust.

4.Success measured by processes. Established rules and regulations. Focus on tasks instead of people.

All of these analyses of human behavior and motivation have some things in common. They also have some differences. In my experience, no one theory is 100% accurate. Human beings are incredibly complex creatures and defy categorization. In the model that I have outlined for your benefit you will want to identify the style and characteristics that most closely approximates you. I must caution you that you will likely have some traits of several of the categories, but it is likely that one will most closely fit your style. My own style most closely approximates that of the Sanguine in the Socrates model; the Feeler in the Jung model; the Interacting Socializer in the Allesandro model; the Influencer in the Carlson Learning Company model. And yet I am also very analytical, measure my success by results, and value sharing and trust. In short, I cross into several categories. I believe that we all do. The key here is to understand that each person you will ever interact with most likely does have a dominant style. If that style is opposite yours you will generally have a natural disconnect in communicating with them. The best way to use the information on the chart is as follows:

1. Identify the style most closely matching your own
2. Think of people you know and see which quadrant they most easily fall into
3. Analyze how you naturally relate to people who fit easily into the four basic quadrants of behavior. Some you will naturally relate to and others you will have to work at to varying degrees.

Remember that the goal should be to reduce tension and increase communication with everyone you interact with every day. This will allow you the greatest opportunity for experiencing positive emotions in every aspect of your daily life. Your ability to achieve success in all of your goals will be greatly enhanced by your increased ability to easily relate to others.

WHICH OF THE FOUR QUADRANTS MOST CLOSELY REPRESENTS YOUR PERSONALITY?

Fast Paced
Blunt
Direct
Assertive
Domineering

Outgoing
Enjoys Human Interaction
Expressive Personality
Likes Personal Contact
Good Influencer
Main Desire is to be Liked
Stereotypes: Salesman, Trial Lawyer

Hard Charging
Type A Personality
Driving
Main Desire to be in Control
Stereotypes: Scarlet O'Hara
Attila the Hun
The boss from "you know where"

Feelings
People
Right Brain
More Emotional

Subjective   *Objective*

Things
Facts
Left brain
Less emotional

Easygoing
Consensus builder
Agreeable
Facilitator
Amicable
Main Desire is to Cooperate
Stereotype: Secretary

Detailed Thinker
Analytical
Main Desire is to be Right
Stereotypes: Research Scientist, Engineer,
Accountant

Passive
Reserved
Indirect
Slow paced
Yielding

Don't be discouraged if much of this seems confusing. If you've been studying these sciences for years—as I've admitted—you can still learn. But even if this is the first time you've ever thought of how to build quicker rapport, the basics are the key. These you've already learned and practiced as you've gone through the exercises in each chapter thus far.

1. Belief in yourself that people will like and respond to you. If you don't like and love yourself any science you learn about relationship building will be merely role-playing for you. In order to build true, lasting friendships you must believe that you are worthy of the love and respect of others.

2. Taking responsibility onto yourself to make the effort to develop rapport. Remember that you enjoy peace and happiness to the exact degree that you are in control of your life. The responsibility is yours, not the other persons.

3. Finding the positives in others. This goes along with everything you've read thus far about positive thinking, positive thoughts, and positive emotions. Take the time to look for the positives. Everyone has them. Understand going in that every person is looking at you and the rest of his or her world through the filter of his or her own belief system. It's entirely possible that the other person is introverted, shy, or has self-doubts. Maybe they're just in a bad mood today. Maybe they've just been jilted by a lover, or yelled at by their mate. Maybe they are having difficulty managing their own mental states and their own anxieties today.

Maybe somebody just kicked his or her cat. Let me explain what I mean. A particular CEO is having a really bad day because the financial reports just came in and they didn't meet expectations. As a result he calls in the President and chews him out big time. "We need to do better than this!" he snaps. The President now calls in the VP and chews him out. "This performance is entirely unacceptable," he growls. "If you can't get better results than this, I'll have to find someone who can." The VP calls in his managers and gives them all the ultimatum to increase performance or their jobs are on the line as well. One of the managers, Fred, just returns to his office and his wife calls with a question about dinner that evening. Still upset from his meeting with the VP he is short with her. "I can't talk about this right now, Margaret, just take care of it yourself," he snaps. Margaret no sooner hangs up the phone and little Johnny runs in the house. "Mom," he says, "My friend Billy just got the coolest video game, can I have $45 to get one, too?" Mom, still stinging from her conversation with Fred yells, "Darn it, Johnny, aren't you ever happy with what you've got? Just go out and play and leave me alone!" Johnny, upset from being yelled at by his Mom, and frustrated because he feels his needs weren't even considered, goes outside and kicks the cat. The moral of the story is this: Wouldn't it have saved everyone a lot of grief and stress if the CEO had originally just driven over to

Johnny's house and kicked the cat himself?   We've all had our cat kicked haven't we?

    4.   The ability and willingness to listen. My Mom used to tell me, "Son, the good Lord gave us two ears and only one mouth. Learn to use them in that proportion." Regardless of all the science that exists in relationship building and rapport this fundamental understanding always applies. People like people who are interested in their needs and their interests. Do you like people who are always telling you about their needs, their wants, their lives, and never show interest in yours? Most likely your closest friends are those who show genuine interest in you. Taking the time to listen to others is the foundation of every successful relationship. You don't have to study for years to master this one, do you?

    5.   Asking open-ended questions. These are questions that cause others to make conversation and to share their thoughts. An example of an open-ended question is: "Tell me about your hobbies." Actually, this isn't a question at all, but it does require the person to open up. Suppose you'd said, "Do you ski?" Maybe you asked the question because you like to ski and you're hoping you can establish rapport. But, what if the other person doesn't like to ski? Suppose they just say, "No." Then what do you do? Or even if they do like to ski, what if they just answer, "Sometimes." Now what do you do? Closed ended questions are those that can be answered with one word. Yes, no, maybe, sometimes, etc. Open ended questions or statements are those that require the other person to open up and converse. Develop the habit of asking open-ended questions, and taking the time to listen to the answers.

Your assignment for today is to identify which style in the chart most closely matches your own. Think about several people you know: Some who you really click with, and others who you just can't seem to get along with no matter what. In my experience those that I have the greatest difficulty establishing rapport with are those on the exact opposite quadrant from my own. I establish instant rapport with those most closely matching my own style. Those on the same side of one axis as my own I can normally establish a rapport, but with a little bit more effort than those in my own quadrant. Spend some time putting names into categories and see if any of this makes sense for you. The next chapter will give you some additional insights in establishing rapport immediately with anyone whether you know which quadrant they fall into or not. Have fun, and I'll see you tomorrow.

Chapter Twenty four

Matching and Mirroring

Wasn't it eye-opening to understand why you click so easily with some people and find it so hard to get along with others? It's almost as if you're speaking a different language with some people, isn't it? In some ways you are. Even the term "body language" implies this. If you've ever traveled to a foreign country or experienced the frustration of trying to understand someone who literally speaks a different language—or have him or her understand you—you may have wished you could speak their language. This chapter is designed to show you how you can quickly and easily speak someone else's body language—especially after some practice. The more time you spend with the chart in the previous chapter the more revelations that will reveal themselves to you about relationships you've struggled with in the past, or may be struggling with currently. Some personality types do not fit as easily in one of the four quadrants as others. That's because most of us as we've matured have learned to style-flex just to get along with people. Style-flexing means adapting your style to more closely approximate that of another person. Most of us have learned to do this over the years without even being consciously aware of it. Especially those of us who have had to adapt to others in a professional work environment have learned to mask our real personalities to some extent to reduce tension and increase harmony. I know engineers and accountants who have trained themselves to be able to put on a charming sales personality even though their natural tendencies are towards the colder, less open style of the lower right quadrant. They have adapted their style to allow them to move up the corporate ladder. This chapter is designed to give you the tools to do it consciously to maximize its effectiveness.

How do you enter another's world?

It's important to understand that gaining rapport is critical in the beginning of relationships more than it will be later on. The more we learn about someone the less our perceptions of them are based on the now. Once someone has gained your trust and confidence you are naturally more forgiving of their momentary lapses of judgment, temperament, or attitude. These criteria can be huge, however, for your judging someone who you've just met—and for their judgment of you. If you are a parent you can easily identify with the following experience. You and your young child—two or three years old—are in a fairly nice restaurant having dinner. Your child begins to throw a temper tantrum. Maybe he/she doesn't like the food, or is just cranky. People begin to look at you in that way that says, "Would you please do something with your child?" What do you do? The point of this example is not to give you advice on child rearing, but to make a point. Your perception of your child is much different from the others around you, wouldn't you agree? Maybe your child's erratic behavior is extremely rare. My son, for example, was a fairly well behaved child. I can remember one experience though, when he was about two years old, where we were on vacation and having dinner at a nice restaurant. For whatever reason he was impossible. He threw his food; he screamed and threw a temper tantrum. Nothing my wife and I did could calm him down. This began just as our food was being served. I'm quite sure the patrons seated anywhere near us thought we had the brattiest child on the planet, and yet we knew that this behavior was not typical at all. They were not equating his behavior as a mere speed bump on an otherwise smooth road. For them the speed bump of the now was the only road they knew, and they didn't like it. Let's change the scene for a moment. In this scene you're at a family function—let's say a family reunion. The other people around you are the child's grandparents, and close family who have known him since birth. How would they view his outburst now? Instead of anger, or disgust as to how his outburst was affecting their meal they might now be concerned about him. What was causing this normally sweet boy to act this way? Was he sick? Was he in some kind of pain?

You know now that your entire perception of the world around you is based on your belief system about yourself and the world around you. The same is true of everyone else. Most of this book has focused on you—how to change your self-beliefs and your beliefs about the world around you to advantage you and help you accomplish your goals—both personal and financial. By now you hopefully have altered your personal belief system to give you much greater self-esteem and greater expectations for your future. None of us lives in a vacuum, however. Unless you are a total hermit your happiness, success, and ability to achieve the future you desire is greatly dependent on others.

AUDITORIES

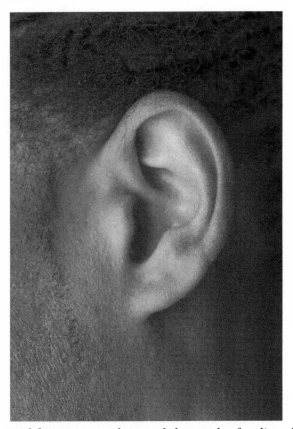

It is critical for you to understand that each of us literally lives in our own little world. All the information we take in about the world around us comes through our five senses. These five senses are sight, hearing, touch, taste, and smell. Of course, you already knew that. But, each of us uses these senses in slightly different ways. For some of us, our hearing is the key sense we utilize to gain information about our world—these are called auditories. Some of us are more visually oriented—these people are called "visuals." For some, it is the sense of touch—these we call "kinesthetics."

VISUALS

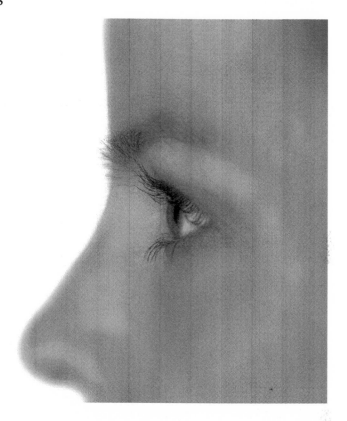

Others are more focused on taste and smell—"gustatories." Unless we have a physical disability we use all five senses to gather data about the world, but each of us is more inclined to one or more of our senses than the others. We also utilize these senses differently at different times. The data that enters through our senses goes into our brains and is filtered through our internal belief system. John Grinder, in his research into Neuro-linguistic programming, called this the meta-model. It's not important that you remember the name, but it is important that you understand that your interpretation of the information coming into your brain through your five senses is only a representation of the true world.

Editing allows in only certain data, and deletes that which is inconsistent with your internal beliefs

Just as a map is a representation of a piece of land, your interpretation of the world around you isn't that true world—it's only the way you see it. I know this sounds strange at first—it did to me. But think about it for a moment. If you go back to the picture of the old hag/young woman in Chapter Two, you already know that your interpretation of that picture is unique to you. The picture exists in its own reality, but you see it differently than others do. Doesn't it make sense that if you want to gain instant rapport with another you can accomplish this much more readily if you're looking at the same world?

How do we gain access to the world of others? We've discussed how your physiology is representative of your mental states. We also know that you can change the way you feel by changing your physiology. Your physiology is a form of communication to others. Just what is communicated to others is determined by their interpretation of your physiology. I was taught early on in my sales career that I should never cross my arms when talking with a customer because this particular physiology would be interpreted as a "closed personality," or an attitude of stubbornness or indifference. I was also taught that my handshake should be very firm, and that I should even pull the hand of the customer/prospect towards me as I shook their hand. I was supposed to establish a very direct eye contact and maintain that eye contact throughout the sales call. These sales strategies are still being taught today in many circles. Unfortunately, they are dead wrong. Although some might interpret your arms folded across your chest as closed or indifferent attitudes, others might interpret them totally differently. I know some people who cross their arms just for comfort, and others who do this when they are reflecting on a particular suggestion or idea. Although some people respond favorably to direct eye contact, others may find it intrusive and overly bold. Some could be very offended by your efforts to "take control" of the sales call by pulling their hand towards you with a very firm handshake, while others may be impressed by this approach. It is ignorant and unproductive to assume that each person reacts the same way to your personality. That is exactly why you establish instant rapport with some people and instantly alienate others with your natural personality style.

You may be the Popeye type; you know, "I am what I am." But think with me here; while Popeye got along great with Olive Oil, he sure didn't click with Bluto. You may have heard the song *I gotta be me*. It goes like this:

I gotta be me
I gotta be me
What else could I be but what I am

If you think that fits your style, you may want to think about it again. I'm not suggesting here that you try to be something you're not. But, I am suggesting that if you want to get along better with others and get what you want out of relationships and out of life, it works much better if you make the effort to enter the worlds of those around you. Once you've established rapport you can eventually gravitate more towards your own natural personality style. One of the principal elements we have worked hard to establish for you in these pages is the personal belief that "I am responsible for every event in my life." Hopefully by now you have embraced that as your own personal philosophy. In like manner, if you take responsibility for how well you relate to other people in every area of your life the results may truly astound you.

You, no doubt, have heard, "You never get another chance to make a first impression." In the case of rapport this couldn't be more accurate. The best way to make a good first impression on someone is what we call "mirroring." Just as the name implies, mirroring is duplicating as close as you can another person's physiology. As we've mentioned, "body language" really is a form of communication or language. It says something to the other person based on their own personality style and their personal belief system. You can mirror a person's physiology by carefully watching the way they are sitting or standing and position your body the same way.   If you are not close enough to them to see or hear their breathing pattern this may be the only thing you can readily mirror. If this is an unfamiliar concept for you, please don't practice it during an important sales call, a job interview, or a meeting with your boss. Practice this method in a park or some public place with people you don't know. You may be surprised how quickly you can gain rapport. If they have their arms folded across their chest, you do the same. If their leg is crossed over the other, you do likewise. This may seem trivial but it works.

The closer you are to an individual the more things you can notice in their physiology. For instance, what is their breathing pattern like—is it high or low in their chest? How fast is it? Try to pattern the pace of your speech to theirs. If they talk loud and fast, your speech should approximate their tempo and volume. You may be afraid that mimicking them will offend them, but this rarely is the case. Very rarely is the person aware of their speech patterns, breathing patterns, and their body language. Just to make sure, though, practice this in low impact situations until you get good at it. Don't try it with your boss until you have confidence that you understand the subtleties of the process.   Remember that instant rapport is generated between people who have like physiology. Later on in the relationship other factors become much more important, such as trust, honesty, integrity, common likes and dislikes, etc. Initially, however, you don't know any of these things about them, nor they about you.

There are four types of mirroring that can be effective in gaining rapport. They can be used individually, or in combinations depending on the situation. They are:

1. Obvious physiology such as posture, crossing of legs, and/or arms, and eye contact.
2. Voice - tone, tempo, volume, pitch, pace.
3. Rhythm movements
4. Breathing patterns

If you're talking with someone on the phone your easiest choice is to match the tone and tempo of your voice with the other persons. Don't exactly try to mimic them as this could backfire. But, if you are a fast talker and the person on the other end is a slow talker try to slow down your tempo. If they talk softly, lower your volume somewhat. If the reverse happens to be true, maybe you need to speed up somewhat and talk a little louder. Believe me, this all felt strange to me at first as well. But it works—that's the key. It's become somewhat of a cliché that the fast talking New Yorker and the slow talking southerner with a drawl are almost talking a different language. There can be instant friction between them—at least until other factors become known between them that can overcome the initial cultural barriers. In truth, though, New Yorkers have many different personality styles, which are reflected in their speech patterns. Southerners don't necessarily talk slower, nor do they necessarily drawl—whatever that means. The key here is to listen carefully to the voice on the other end. If they are talking fast—to your mind—try speeding up your natural pace. Don't try to talk with a southern accent if you're a native New Yorker, but if the person at the other end is talking slower, try slowing your speech patterns down to approximate theirs.

Matching another's breathing rate is very effective if you're in close proximity. It's also very subtle and effective. You can notice their breathing rate by the movement in their chest or abdomen. Watching the edge of the person's shoulder silhouetted against a background is also effective. If you think this sounds silly, why not try it in different situations for awhile before you dismiss the idea totally. You may be surprised by the result. As I mentioned earlier, my early training in sales was almost the exact opposite of these techniques. Although I was quite successful in selling, I believe now that much of my training limited my success instead of helped. I succeeded in spite of the training, not because of it. I used to wonder why I had such difficulty establishing rapport with certain prospects, but since I learned these techniques I can establish rapport almost instantly with anyone. It's almost impossible to convince someone of your point of view if they feel irritated by your mere presence.

Recently I had a sales call with the Vice President of Technical Services of a large company. I brought the product manager of my company along to answer any technical questions that I might not be able to answer and also to impress this important customer with our commitment to him and his company. I could tell almost instantly that my normal personality style and that of my prospect were not in sync. His handshake was not firm, nor was his demeanor particularly friendly. He directed us to sit in the chairs on the other side of his desk, as he sat behind it. He slumped in his chair; his arms and legs crossed, and seemed somewhat disinterested in what I had to say. He did not seem to want to make direct eye contact. In the old days I would have attempted to get physically close to this man, and establish a strong eye contact. In this case, I did just the opposite. I consciously attempted to slump in my seat—not a natural thing to do on a sales call. I also crossed my arms and legs and made intermittent eye contact. My approach was much more casual and less professional than I would have ever been in my natural state. Before long, this man barely looked at my partner. He eventually came from behind his desk and sat directly across from me and began to make very good eye contact with me. His entire demeanor changed from one of disdain to one of attention and sincere interest. Quickly we had a rapport that I believe I never would have made with the old sales approach. The call went very well and we got permission to sell our products throughout his company. I ask you: Did I degrade myself in any way by making the effort to enter his world? I think not. Was I being phony by trying to act differently than my natural style? Again, I don't think so at all. What I did do was gain an instant rapport with a tough prospect and succeeded in my sales objectives. I don't believe that I misled him in anyway by consciously acting somewhat different than my natural personality style. If I were traveling in a foreign country and had the ability to communicate in the language of the natives you better believe I would. I guarantee I would make more friends, build better rapport, and have a lot more fun than if I couldn't effectively communicate with those around me. Entering another's world with these methods is no different than learning to speak someone else's language—and it's a whole lot easier to learn.

Your assignment for today is to practice these techniques in a low-impact environment such as the shopping mall, the park, anywhere that you can interact with people you don't yet know. If you want to get daring you can try it with people you have had difficulty connecting with in the past. See if your new mirroring techniques open up some doors that were previously closed for you. Have fun, and I'll see you tomorrow.

CHAPTER TWENTY-FIVE

DESTRUCTIVE ADDICTIVE BEHAVIORS

How do you feel about slavery? This may seem a strange question, but believe it or not even in the United States of America today there are still millions of slaves. The same is true in every country of the world whether democratic, dictatorship, socialist, or communist. Incredible you say. You don't believe me? What if I was to tell you that you might be one of them? Now you really don't believe me do you? The World Book Dictionary's second definition of a slave—right after a person who is owned by another—is as follows: "A person who is *controlled* or ruled by some desire, habit, or influence." Webster's Dictionary, in its second definition says an addict is a slave. It is imperative in your growth, as a human being and your quest to be all you are capable of being that you analyze your life right now and see if you fit this definition. We are happy and at peace with ourselves to the exact degree that we are in control of our own lives. Throughout mankind's history, no matter how well treated slaves were by their masters they eventually fought for their freedom—they needed to control their own lives. To Americans, freedom is considered to be a fundamental human right. In fact, we treasure freedom above all others. If some desire, habit, or influence *controls* you, or you are an addict, you are not truly free, are you?

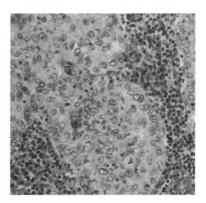

CANCER CELLS – ULTIMATE SELFISHNESS?

In my experience destructive addictive behaviors are also selfish behaviors. Addictive behaviors focus on immediate self-gratification without thought or concern for others. Selfishness may be the most devastating force in human history. The purest example I can think of for selfishness is the cancer cell. What the cancer cell does is rob the healthy cells around it of life giving nutrients. Scientists don't know what causes cancer although there are many theories including viral infection of some sort. What scientists do know is that what had been normal healthy cells mutate and begin to replicate; robbing more and more nutrients from the healthy cells around them. The cancer cells multiply into the thousands and millions until eventually the host organism dies, with what effect? —The cancer of course dies with them. Selfishness in humanity ultimately causes the same effect. Naturally, we are all selfish to some degree. We've already discussed that every behavior is to avoid pain or gain pleasure. I've even heard arguments—which can border on the absurd—that every human behavior is done for selfish reasons. This argument asserts that the love we give our children makes us feel good and therefore is really given selfishly. When we help others it makes us feel good, and there again is really for selfish gain. My answer to such arguments is okay, if you want to ascribe selfish motives to selfless behaviors, then so be it. You may have heard this: "The way to get everything you want out of life is by helping many others get what they want." This is the kind of selfishness that is beneficial. A more realistic understanding of selfishness, though, is any behavior that is purely for your own gratification with no thought or concern for others. I'm sure you know people who you would describe as selfish. Are these individuals a pleasure to be around? Are they happy? Selfishness is self-destructive and is one of the biggest causes of the problems in the world today. As long as people are only interested in their own gratification, problems will be caused for those around them. Where ordinary selfish behavior can become addictive is when the primary focus becomes the now.

I recently came across a story that depicts selfishness very well, and why giving of yourself to others is not only loving, but ultimately beneficial to you as well.

A man was having a conversation with God one day and said, "God, I would like to know what the difference is between The Light of your Truth and The Darkness of Satan? "

He was then led to two doors. He opened one of the doors and looked in. In the middle of the room was a large round table. In the middle of the table was a large pot of stew, which smelled delicious and made the man's mouth water.

The people sitting around the table were thin and sickly. They appeared to be famished. They were holding spoons with very long handles that were strapped to their arms and each found it possible to reach into the pot of stew and take a spoonful.

But because the handle was longer than their arms, they could not get the spoons back into their mouths. The man shuddered at the sight of their misery and suffering.

God said, 'You have seen The Darkness.'

They went to the next room and opened the door. It was exactly the same as the first one.

There was the large round table with the large pot of stew which made the man's mouth water. The people were equipped with the same long-handled spoons, but here the people were well nourished and plump, laughing and talking.

The man said, 'I don't understand.'

It is simple,' said God. 'It requires but one skill. You see they have learned to feed each other, while the greedy think only of themselves.'

You may have already heard the true story of the best way to catch a monkey. You put something in a glass jar that the monkey really wants like a fig or something particularly tasty with an opening only large enough to get his hand in. When the monkey grabs hold of the fig his fist is too large to pull out of the hole. The monkey will grab hold of his prize and be trapped because he refuses to let go of the fig. All he has to do to gain his freedom is to release the prize. How many of us get trapped by our greed, or selfishness and refuse to let go even if it means our very lives?

Some of the behaviors I will list as addictive may surprise you, but I believe if you really think about them you will agree that they fit the definition above. Some are worse than others, but remember again that as long as you are controlled by your behaviors you are not totally in control of your own life—it's that simple. Webster's Dictionary defines an addict as "Someone who is a slave to a habit." It also says that if you are a slave to a habit "you are addicted." Before you read the behaviors that I am convinced can qualify as addictive I would like you to make your own list. What habits or behaviors can cause you to lose control over your own life? Please take the time to make your own list below.

Now, I'd like to you take a look at my list and see how many behaviors we agree are; or at least can become addictive.
1. Drinking alcohol
2. Tobacco (cigarettes, cigars, chewing tobacco, etc.)
3. Taking drugs (which can include prescription drugs).
4. Taking into your body by any method (through the nose, mouth, intravenous, etc.) any mind altering substance
5. Sex (by the way, oral sex is definitely sex)
6. Masturbation
7. Pornography (reading it, watching it, listening to it, participating in it)
8. Food
9. Gambling

You probably included alcohol, drug use, and smoking on your list. These are behaviors that just about everyone admits are—or at least can be—addictive. Do sex, masturbation, and pornography surprise you? Most scientists today will agree that sex can become an addiction, and masturbation is one form of sex. Is the act done for instant gratification with the focus purely on self? It would be hard to argue that certain sexual activities don't fit this definition precisely. Pornography is normally a driver and a contributor in sexual abuse and pedophilia. Sexual acts release extremely powerful endorphins that are the most pleasurable the body is capable of producing on its own. If people can be addicted to nicotine, alcohol, even caffeine, then it's silly to say that people can't be addicted to sex, which is far more pleasurable. In fact, for most humans the orgasm is the most intense experience of momentary pleasure ever attained. We know that we become what we think about. As Zig Ziglar says, "You are what you feed your mind." In the case of pornography and masturbation, what are you feeding your mind? Webster's dictionary defines selfishness as "devoted only to oneself." Doesn't masturbation fit that description? Selfishness is a negative emotion and therefore attracts more negative thoughts and emotions in our lives. My own experience has taught me that the more we train ourselves to focus on the needs and pleasures of others the more love we receive in return, and the greater the quality of our relationships.

Although it is necessary for us to eat, food can become addictive if we use it to somehow make up for something else in our lives that is missing. If we eat to make ourselves feel better when we're depressed we can be headed in the wrong direction. Another sign we may be losing control is when we binge and then feel guilty or ashamed afterwards.

Gambling causes some to lose complete control over their lives. These individuals will spend every cent they can get their hands on in pursuit of that rush of adrenaline that they may have once gotten from a big win. You may know people who have lost their families, their jobs, and their self-respect this way. Over time almost nobody comes out ahead—except the house. Remember that they didn't build those gorgeous casinos in Las Vegas and Atlantic City on the money they made from winners.

One way to determine whether you are addicted to something is to stop doing it for at least thirty days and see how your body reacts. If you go through withdrawal which is pretty easy to identify you are definitely addicted. But you don't have to go through withdrawal in order to be addicted. If after a few days a particular behavior is pretty much all you can think about, you are probably addicted to it. Ask yourself the question once again, "Am I in control of the behavior, or is the behavior in control of me?" If you find yourself hiding your behavior from others—particularly your loved ones—this may be another telltale sign of addiction.

We have spent a great deal of time in this book discussing how to develop the right habits of thinking, and certainly these habits can become addicting to the point where you really love doing them. If you stop doing them you will miss the rush of positive energy and the highs you experience from focusing your mind's energies in the right direction. Many say that they are addicted to exercise. You may even become addicted—in a figurative sense—to positive books, tapes, and seminars. In fact, in the last chapter of this book I will encourage you to develop these habits to help you continue on your road to personal growth and development. Certainly these behaviors are not destructive ones generally. But, even these behaviors can become destructive if you become so focused on them that you no longer are in control of your life.

You may have listed some behaviors that I didn't include—that's okay. As we've mentioned, any behavior can become destructive if we lose control over it. To help you identify which behaviors are positive (constructive) and which are negative (destructive) I have put together a list of ten questions for you to ask yourself. It's important that you be totally honest with yourself, as addictive behaviors can easily cloud your judgment and allow you to rationalize almost anything if you get enough immediate pleasure from it.

1. Does the behavior have positive or negative effects on me today?
2. If this behavior turns into a habit what will its long-term effects be on my life?
3. Is the behavior in harmony with my life's goals?
4. Does the behavior make it easier or harder for me to develop meaningful relationships with others?
5. Am I doing this for instant self-gratification, and only for me? Addictive behaviors are done for me, me, me; now, now, now!
6. If I continue this behavior, especially if I do it more frequently, what effect will it have on my health now, and in the future?
7. Does the behavior make me feel good about myself?

8. Is the behavior helpful or detrimental to me becoming the person I want to be?
9. Does this behavior allow me to feel more or less positive emotions each day?
10. If I continue this behavior long-term, will it have positive or negative effects on those around me, particularly those I love?

WHAT ARE THE ROAD SIGNS ALONG THE WAY?

Your assignment for today is to put any behavior or habit that you either have or are thinking about starting to the test of these ten questions. Take yourself into the future as you did during your goal setting exercises and see whether the behavior looks good or bad for others and yourself. You remember the drill. You are now old and wise. Reflect back on your life as you picture your life with the habit, and then without the habit. Make the visualizations as real as you possibly can. See the colors, hear the sounds, smell the smells. How do you feel about yourself with the habit as part of your life? How do you feel about yourself and your life without the habit having been a part of it? How has your habit affected your loved ones and others around you? What have their lives been like as a result of your habit?

Think of these ten questions as landmarks that should be clearly visible for you along the road you have chosen for your life. If you don't see the right landmarks you know you have taken a wrong turn. When this happens, if you don't turn around and get back on the right route, you will end up where you didn't want to go. If you don't like what you see, you owe it to yourself and your loved ones to end your destructive addictive behaviors now. List the steps you will take beginning today to end your addiction. A great way to break the mold of selfishness and addictive patterns is to give unselfishly to others and make that a habit instead.

197

1.
2.
3.
4.
5.

Write down all the reasons you must take these steps beginning today.

1.
2.
3.
4.
5.

Now, write down all the positive benefits that will be realized by taking these steps beginning now.

1.
2.
3.
4.
5.

I'll see you tomorrow.

Chapter Twenty-six

What your Mom may have told you

Old cliches which can change your life

ll of us grew up hearing "words of wisdom" that we mostly ignored. We may have ignored them because from a child's perspective we weren't able to make the connections to life that revealed the quality of their basic truth. Or, we might have ignored them because we didn't understand what they meant. Even if we didn't ignore them we most likely swore to ourselves that we'd never say the same things when we had kids of our own. As I write this I have two grown up daughters and one son who is thirteen. I have to admit that I have caught myself saying these same things to my own children many times. Somehow they make much more sense than they did when I was growing up.

A rose with thorns;

Or, thorns with a rose?

The reason I want to review them here is because I believe it's important for you to appreciate that the training we've gone through together in the pages of this book is fundamental truth at a very basic level. Let's review some of the things our parents may have tried to teach us. See if you remember any of these "oldies but goodies."

Count your blessings: If your Mom didn't tell you this every time you asked for the latest new toy on the market she wasn't like my Mom. By asking yourself the "five for ten" questions every morning and every night you have hopefully developed this wonderful habit of training your mind to dwell on what's right in your life. The "five for ten" questions are:

1. Who do I love and who loves me?
2. What one thing about myself do I really like? —Or, What am I most proud of in my life right now?
3. What three things in my life right now do I get the most joy from?
4. What can I do today to have some fun? The nighttime question is "What can I do tomorrow to have some fun?
5. What can I do today/tomorrow to bring joy to someone else?

Two wrongs don't make a right: Even though it doesn't say it, the implication here is that we would forgive instead of retaliate. Remember that in order to release the brakes on the emotions that hold us back we must forgive everyone freely, including ourselves.

Do you look at the glass as half empty or half full? We've often been told that if we look at life in a positive way we would see the glass as half full. I've also heard it said, "Does a rose have thorns; or do thorns have roses?" I'm sure you know people who can brighten up any room---just by leaving it! They certainly could benefit from this one, and the next one, which says:

Find a silver lining in every cloud: Do you know anyone who can find a cloud in every silver lining? Are they fun to be around?

CLOUD, OR A SILVER LINING?

Treat others like you want them to treat you: This is a quote from the Bible, which says, "Do unto others as you would have them do unto you." Love is one emotion that we can't give enough of. The more we give the more we receive from others.

Try to find the good in others: I've also heard it said, "Focus on the person and not on the blemishes." We've all got blemishes, haven't we? This goes along with the next one, which says:

You attract more flies with honey than you do with vinegar: By being nice to others we make a lot of friends and allies who can help us achieve our goals.

If you can't say something nice about someone, don't say anything at all: Trash talking someone behind his or her back generally comes back to haunt us. The real winners in life find a way to take the high road. Have you ever wondered: When someone is trash talking another behind his/her back what do they say about you behind yours?

When you point a finger at someone else, you have four fingers pointing back at you: Accepting responsibility is the biggest element in gaining control over our own lives.

The *"Serenity Prayer"*: *Lord, grant me the serenity to accept the things I can't change, the courage to change the things I can, and the wisdom to know the difference.* Can anyone argue with the logic of this classic prayer?

Get your attitude right: Zig Ziglar calls a negative attitude, "Hardening of the attitude." Brian Tracey calls it "Psychosclerosis." I call it "Attitusclerosis." People that don't have the right attitude always seem to have a *"chip on their shoulder."*

Can't never did anything but lay in a ditch: I used to hate this one when my Mom said it to me. Winners never make excuses. Winners take action!

Don't make a mountain out of a molehill: A friend of mine told me a story about his ex-neighbor—a very nice man in his early 70's—who died recently. What had happened was this: A young girl tried to buy a bicycle at his garage sale for $4 less than he was asking. When he refused, her grandmother came by an hour later in her new Cadillac and pleaded that her granddaughter only had $21, not the $25 he was asking. He became so incensed at the woman that he had a heart attack and died the next day.

Another example of making mountains out of molehills is road rage. Learn to let the other motorist have his/her way if it's so important to them. Let them go on, and out of your life. Making an issue out of a road incident can get you seriously hurt, or even killed.

We need goals: Our lives always move in the direction of our dominant thoughts. You now have written goals, which focus your thoughts on the direction that you have chosen; as opposed to the direction others choose for you.

A calm heart is the life of the fleshly organism: Anxiety and stress are damaging to your peace of mind, and to your health.

To err is human, to forgive divine: Enough said.

No doubt, you may be able to come up with more than these. Maybe our parents weren't so dumb after all.

HOW ABOUT SOME OTHER SAPPY SENTIMENTS TO GO ALONG WITH THE OLD CLICHES?

What if love ruled the world?

Do you remember the words to John Lennon's landmark song *Imagination*? You may remember the theme—a world with no war, where people of all races and nationalities would get along in peace. One verse, which I feel captures the idea best of all, is:

You may say I'm a dreamer
But I'm not the only one
I hope someday you'll join us
And the world will live as one

As you look around at what is happening in the world today do you ever wonder why there is so much hate and divisiveness? What would the world be like if love—positive emotion at its purest—and the emotions that go along with it did prevail?

Love
Joy
Peace
Goodness
Mildness
Faith
Patience
Confidence
Selflessness
Self-control
Up-building

If you turn on the evening news or watch CNN there isn't a great deal going on in the world that focuses on these positives is there?

What would change if everyone asked himself/herself the following questions each day?

- If everyone treated his or her friends and family the way I treat mine would the world be a better or a worse place for us all to live in?
- If everyone dealt with those around them the way I do would things improve, get worse, or stay the same?
- Would the world have more or less hatred if everyone were like me?

- Would there be more or fewer wars?
- Would there be more or less crime?
- Would there be a need for more or less prisons?
- Would people feel safer on the streets or more in fear than they are already?
- Would there be more or fewer lawsuits if everyone conducted business the way I do?
- Would the environment in which our progeny will spend their lives be more preserved or more destroyed if everyone were like me?
- Would there be more or less divisiveness if everyone had the same attitudes about themselves and others as I do?

Another question to ask yourself is "What am I leaving behind?" In Stephen Covey's *First Things First* he talks about the four priorities we should have in our lives—To Live, To Love, To Learn, To Leave a Legacy. We're all going to leave some legacy. What kind of world will you be leaving to your heirs? What will people that knew you say about you after you're gone? Ask yourself the question, "If I died today would the world be better or worse off from my having lived in it?"

WHAT WILL YOUR LEGACY BE?

I believe that if everyone asked themselves these questions on a regular basis, maybe John Lennon's vision wouldn't be such a crazy fantasy after all. We can ask ourselves each day, "Am I building bridges, or am I tearing them down," and "Was I the best person I could be today?" Each day is a new opportunity, isn't it?

I may sound like a sentimental fool to some but I don't care. I recently watched a film I hadn't seen in a while. The film is called *Scrooged*. It's a modern remake of *A Christmas Carol*. In it Bill Murray plays a TV Executive who is abusive to his friends, his family, those who work for him, and even to the one woman in his life he supposedly loves.

Even though he's very successful financially he is not a happy guy. I'm sure you know the story of Scrooge in *A Christmas Carol* so I won't go through all the details, but after the Christmas Eve visions with the ghosts of Christmas past, present, and future, he wants to have every day be Christmas Eve. Not the real Christmas Eve, but the ideal most people would like it to be, with everyone being loving and caring to everyone around them. What would your world be like if all the people around you treated you this way? We can't control the people around us, but we can control ourselves.

Here's another crazy idea. How would the world be changed for the better if we all viewed every day as Thanksgiving? Not the Thanksgiving that the day has become, but what it was originally when the Pilgrims and Indians—two different races and cultures—got together to truly give thanks for the simple blessings they had in their lives. How your life would be changed if you asked yourself every morning and every night what you had to be thankful for.

Can you think of anyone that you personally know whom you believe "has it made," and yet they are still unhappy? Now turn that question around and ask yourself whether you find yourself ever feeling sorry for yourself instead of focusing on the joys that are right in front of you that you take for granted.

Your assignment for today is to become Scrooge after experiencing all-night visions of Christmas past, Christmas present, and Christmas future and waking up to find that it isn't too late to make it right for yourself and those around you. Your past is behind you, and today begins an opportunity to begin a new life—your second chance. Just for today I want you to greet everyone you meet as if you've just found a long lost friend. Go up to everyone at the office or wherever you will be today and greet each person with a friendly smile. Find something good in every person—believe me, it's there if you look for it. Even those you may not normally like; just for today treat them as dear friends who you care deeply about. Treat your wife, husband, or significant other as you did when you were first dating, when you were doing everything in your power to make a great impression. Let all bygones be bygones as they say just for today. "Crazy," you say, "Dennis has really lost it this time!" Why not try it? You may be very surprised at the reactions you get from those you normally wouldn't give the time of day, or those you thought were your enemies. You just might find you enjoy living this way so much that you'll want to continue living your life this way. Hey, what have you got to lose? Have fun showing others what a great person you can be. I'll see you tomorrow.

Chapter Twenty-Seven

Worry

Worry is negative goal setting. When you worry, you allow your mind to dwell on potentially pain causing events that may or may not happen to you in the future. Worry is very closely identified with doubt, and fear. When you allow worry to enter your mind, what is in control? Wherever uncertainty reigns in your mind and heart, you are not in control of your life and your emotions. We have said many times that you are at happy and at peace to the exact degree that you are in control of your own life. In order to worry you must allow negative thoughts into your mind, and the negative emotions that come with them. Remember what sticks—like flypaper—to negative thoughts and emotions? That's right, other negative thoughts and emotions. These thoughts drive away the positive thoughts, limit your creativity, and rob you of your joy and peace of mind. Okay you say, "I'm convinced I shouldn't worry, but I can't help myself." My answer to that is "Yes you can."

Since worry is caused by the uncertainty of an outcome, the way to erase it is by making the outcome certain. Once the outcome is certain, you take control, allowing calm to come into your mind. Studies have shown that your worst fears—essentially the foundation of your worry—very seldom happen. In order to erase worry from your life you must act like the worst has happened, and then make plans so that it doesn't. If that sounds crazy to you—and I admit that it did to me at first—try it. For any situation that you are worried about, write down your worst fears—what's the worst thing that can happen? This is the root cause of your worry, lurking around a dark corner in your mind. Basically, worry is a fear of the unknown.

Once you have identified that unknown, it's seldom as scary as you imagined it. When you write it down you must understand that statistically the worst very seldom happens. Then, write down the best outcome that could happen. The way to do this is by taking a clean sheet of paper and drawing a line vertically down the middle. On the right side of the paper write the heading *Worst Case Scenario*. On the left side of the paper, write *Best Case Scenario*. Write these two versions of the future down in detail. What are the negative effects of your worst case scenario? What are the positive effects of your best case scenario? Now—and this is the key—put together an action plan for making the outcome fit your best case scenario. By doing this, you have taken the control. An action plan once again is a list of steps, which you will follow, in logical order to accomplish a positive outcome. What will you do first? What will you do second? What will you do third? —And so on.

You will find that in most cases taking action to make your positive outcome a reality will immediately focus your mind on positives. Remember that winners take action, losers wait for something to happen to them. You are a winner.

Your assignment for today is to go through this process at least once. If you are worrying about more than one thing, I would advise you to go through this process for every worry you are dragging around—like excess baggage—with you. Remember that to release the brakes of your full potential you must develop the habits of thinking only positive thoughts. I have some fun with this sometimes where I visualize my mind as a den of solitude, my special place. There is a high fence around my mind with a large sign on the fence telling the outside world, "Only positives allowed herein." This works for me. Maybe it will work for you, too.

Serenity Prayer

Have you ever heard the "Serenity Prayer?" Think with me for a second about the word—serenity. What does it mean to you? Do you think of a feeling of peacefulness, calm, maybe joy? Wouldn't you like to feel serenity, especially at the times your life may feel like it's spinning out of control? Control is the key. The "Serenity Prayer" goes something like this: *Lord, grant me the serenity to accept the things I can't change, the courage to change the things I can, and the wisdom to know the difference.* Doesn't this really mean controlling the things you can and not worrying about the things you can't? We have discussed the importance of taking responsibility for your own life, and that the degree we feel peace and joy in our lives is in direct proportion to how much we feel in control. However, it's important to realize that there is much in this world that we cannot control. For example, I can't control the stock market. It goes up and down, seemingly without logic much of the time. I've always found it interesting that when the results of yesterday's stock fluctuations are written in the paper there always is an analysis according to some "expert" of why it did what it did. Interestingly, though, if you ask three different experts you may get three different opinions. If you subscribe to any of the magazines which offer expert advice on investments you may have noticed that while one expert is suggesting you should buy, another expert is advising you to sell. Most financial advisers who make their living analyzing and making investments don't beat the S&P 500, which is just an index of the top 500 stock companies in the US. Now, if you are the CEO or CFO of your company you can certainly influence the value of your company's stock, but you can't control all the events that affect it, such as the world economy, or currency fluctuations. None of us—with the possible exception of Alan Greenspan—can control the market, however.

I am not writing this in an attempt to offer investment counseling, but merely to suggest that much of what happens to us really is beyond our direct control. It makes no sense, therefore, to worry about things over which we have no control. You may say, "Wait a minute here, how can I not worry about the stock market going down when I have my money invested in it?" Let me ask you a question in return, "Does your worrying about it change anything?" If you're so worried about it you owe it to yourself to put your money into safer more conservative investments. My philosophy is that I'm in the market for the long haul. I know it's going to go up and down, many days for no apparent reason. I have my money in what I have researched to be good long-term investments and I know that over time the market will continue to rise. It always has. Those who jumped off tall buildings during the crash of 1929 would have made all their money back if they just waited a couple of years. I say again, by worrying over things you have no control you deprive yourself of the energy to change for the better the things you can control. You also allow negative thoughts and emotions to rule your life.

Do you, for example, have anything to do with whether the countries which made up the former Soviet Union take proper care of the weapons of mass destruction which were stockpiled during the Cold War? If you do, then I beg you to take the proper measures to make sure that World War III isn't started by them falling into the wrong hands. For my part, I can say with certainty that this is something I have no control over at all. Most likely you have nothing to do with it either. So why worry? You might rightly respond, "But if these weapons aren't properly guarded they could fall into the hands of terrorists which could start a horrible war which would cause the death of millions, possibly devastate the world's economy and possibly destroy life on earth as we know it." I agree that this is a possibility, but I must insist, "Can you change this?" If you can, please do. But most likely you can't. It is my firm belief that each of us has only so much energy. If we waste that energy worrying about things we can't control we will not utilize that energy to control the things we can. I can totally control my thoughts, and by so doing I can totally control my actions. I am not saying that it is easy to do this, but only that it can be done. The pages of this book have given you the methods to control your thoughts and by so doing to control your actions. Let me ask you another question, "Can you control the thoughts and actions of any other person other than yourself?" If you believe you can, I would like you to tell me how. Certainly, you can influence the thoughts and behavior of others, but you can't control them. You can, however, totally control your own thoughts and actions. By taking the challenge to do so you begin a new life which can greatly affect the lives of those around you for the better. If enough of us take this responsibility maybe we can change the world after all.

Your assignment for today is to make a list of any worries that have been nagging at your mind. Write it (them) down in detail as we've just discussed. Do your best case and your worst case scenarios. Then put together an action plan—your first action will be today—to make the outcome fit your best case. Do this for every worry you have. Trust me, you'll feel a lot better. I'll see you tomorrow.

Chapter Twenty eight

Ways to Alter Your Mental States

This chapter is designed to help you pick yourself up when you're feeling down. There's an old saying: "When you're up to your butt in alligators it's hard to remember that your original objective was to drain the swamp!" No matter how hard we work at being positive there are some times that life just "gets in the way." We may want to thrive in peace while living in the oasis but sometimes it feels like we're just surrounded by wolves. So far we've discussed many ways on how to keep your mind focused on positive thoughts, giving you positive emotions, and allowing yourself to reap the positive behaviors and results that always follow the right way of looking at yourself and your life. The ways we've outlined include:

1. The "Five for Ten" questions you can ask yourself each night and each morning.

2. Asking yourself the right questions all day long, such as: "What is positive about this that I can use for the benefit of others and myself?" Or, "What can I learn from this to become a better person in the future?" Or, simply, "What is positive about this?" There is always a positive side to everything if we look hard enough for it.

Make someone happy!

3. Practicing your positive visualizations as often as possible of the future you desire. Once again, the most effective way of doing this is by taking yourself to your place of solitude, going through your relaxation techniques, and then making your visualizations as clear and real as is possible. Bring all your senses into play during your visualizations—See the colors and texture, hear the sounds, smell the smells, taste the tastes. Most importantly of all, let yourself feel the joy and satisfaction from the fruits of your labor in achieving your goals. Bring your loved ones into your visualizations and allow yourself the satisfaction of seeing and sharing in the joy your future will bring to them, as well.

4. Re-reading and re-writing your goals. Make this a positive experience, not a punitive one. If your goals are not being met as rapidly as you had hoped, find a way to congratulate yourself on the "baby steps" you've taken in the right direction. Belief and faith are key to your success. If you've had setbacks along the way, don't punish yourself—forgiveness is the positive emotion necessary here—but, analyze where you went wrong and make an action plan to learn from the mistake,

and move once again in the direction you had planned. If you've made great progress towards the realization of your goals it's important that you take the time to celebrate. Buy yourself a special gift or take your significant other out on the town. Celebrate your successes, and forgive yourself for your failures—not forgetting to learn from them.

5. Do something that makes someone else feel good. One of the amazing gifts that we have as human beings is the ability to receive the greatest pleasure from giving selflessly—the opposite of selfishly—for the benefit of others. Get in a volunteer program, for example. Help out the elderly in your neighborhood, or take some gifts to a nursing home in your area. Volunteer for a charity function or something in your religious affiliation that brings joy to others. Call on a sick friend, or just do something special for your wife, husband, children, or significant other.

6. Exercise. Getting yourself moving can quickly get you out of a down frame of mind, as well as allowing your body to release the endorphins that can help to create a sense of well being all on their own.

7. Changing your physiology from a posture of fatigue and depression to one of a positive, enthusiastic outlook can immediately alter your mental state and make you feel better about yourself and your world. Remember that your mind and body are inextricably linked. Your thoughts can affect your physiology, just as your physiology can affect your thoughts. If you're having a hard time getting your thoughts under control at a particular time, try changing your physiology.

FEEL LIKE DANCING?

    In addition to these areas, there are a few more suggestions that I have for you:

    Listen to some good music. Music is one of the most powerful mood altering forces available for humans. William Congreve, in his *Hymn to Harmony*—written over 300 years ago—said: "Music alone with sudden charms can bind the wandering sense, and calm the troubled mind." Ancient Greek writings, written long before this, stated that "musical training is a more potent instrument than any other, because rhythm and harmony find their way into the inward places of the soul." Germany's Nazis used stirring march music to help prepare large crowds for Adolph Hitler's mesmerizing speeches. It is well documented that Hitler's dynamic rhetoric combined with the intoxicating music drove the people into a frenzy of support for his regime.

You no doubt have experienced how a certain melody can instantly transport your thoughts back to a particular time and/or event in your own life without your conscious attempt to do so. Have you ever caught yourself helplessly humming a tune hours or even days after you heard it? Or, have you ever caught yourself singing along with a song on the radio that you hadn't heard in years, and remembering all or most of the words? The TV show *Ally McBeal* hilariously used music to literally transform the personalities of some of its characters. John—normally a boring and shy introvert—becomes a bold romantic when he plays Barry White songs in his head. Ally's therapist, Tracey (played by Tracey Ullman) convinces Ally to pick a special upbeat song to play in her head whenever she feels down or feels encumbered by her own doubts and fears. Tracey Ullman demonstrates how it works by dancing around her office singing her favorite song—*Tracey,* a snappy song from the 70's—at the top of her lungs. Although funny to watch, music can truly have that powerful of an effect on us.

MUSIC STIRS THE SOUL

Anthony Storr, in his book *Music and the Mind*, cites astonishing examples of patients with severe neurological disorders such as Parkinson's disease that could only move after being played tunes they remembered from their youth. If you have any doubts that music can significantly change your mood, think about the last time you went to a wedding reception, or a dance. I'll bet you caught yourself tapping your foot along with songs that you liked, or found yourself dancing almost in spite of yourself. You probably also found yourself covering your ears, or leaving the room when types of music you didn't like were played. I've recently read articles showing that classical music can have a positive effect on the intellectual and emotional development of young children. On the contrary, heavy metal and hard rock music can stimulate aggressive and even violent behavior in some people. The journal *Adolescence* reached the conclusion that "both the adolescents and their parents report significantly more turmoil in the lives of the adolescents who listen to a steady diet of heavy metal and rap music."

Music and language are uniquely human. Music has the ability to reach us at an emotional level more effectively than almost any other form of communication. Try noticing the music playing along with an emotionally moving movie sometime. If it's a violent or sexually graphic film an entirely different kind of music is played than if the mood is more sweet or sentimental. Producers know that the music can create a strong emotional involvement even if the dialogue and/ or acting may be lacking. Movies such as *Sleepless in Seattle* have had their soundtracks sell millions of copies. When I first saw the movie I wasn't even consciously aware of the music. It was only after my daughter bought me the soundtrack that I became aware of the emotional attachment I had to the music, even more than the movie itself.

Advertisers spend millions of dollars creating just the right song or musical background to their product pitches. Few television or radio advertisements are shown without musical accompaniment. This is because the aim of most advertising is to make buying an emotional response rather than a logical one. It has been said that logic and language are left brain functions, while music is a right brain—emotion—function. Logic makes us reason, but emotions move us to act.

People can have different reactions to the same music, as we know. It is not my intention to tell you what music to listen to, however, if you want to create an uplifting feeling of well being, or peace of mind, it is clear that some of the types of music we have just discussed aren't likely to do it for you. I would suggest that you give some thought to what music will create a positive emotional response for you—pick you up, and make you feel happy. The next time you're feeling a little down why not turn on your radio or stereo and give it a try. You might want to take your ipod or mp3 player with you and combine your music with the exercise your body needs anyway. This way you get the positive effects of both working for you at the same time.

Do something different for a change of pace. If you live in the city, try getting out to the country. If you live in the country, why not take a ride into the city? Invite some different people over to dinner than your usual friends. If you eat at the same place for lunch every day, try a different type of cuisine and a different environment. Take a vacation, or just a long weekend. Take your wife, husband, or significant other out for a totally different kind of evening than you normally would. If you normally go casual try really dressing up for a change. If you normally dress up, try going just the opposite.

Get out away from the lights of the city or town you live in and ponder the wonders of the magnificent nighttime sky. Let your mind take you to a totally different awareness from your norm. Allow yourself to wonder at the vastness of the universe and your unique place in it. Take the time to reflect on how truly special you are.

The key is to make it new and different than the "same old, same old." Get out of your rut, break the mold. Remember what my Dad used to say: "You've only got one walk through this veil of tears so you might as well enjoy it!"

Your assignment for today is to do something totally different than you normally do. Plan something exciting, unique, and fun. Do it today.

CHAPTER 29

BIOGRAPHIES

At the age of five, Julio Cuevas's Mom took his two younger brothers back to Puerto Rico and left him with his father and his grandmother in the Hispanic barrios of Brooklyn, NY. Julio explains it this way: "She felt it would be tough enough to support herself and two little boys; Apparently, she thought I had the best chance to make it with Dad."

Grandma spoke no English and Dad wasn't much of a role model for the boy, as he was more concerned with his illegal numbers running business. Julio joined his first gang at the age of eight—more as a means of survival than anything else. It was either join the "Baby Bops," (the little kid subset of the "Big Bops," the real gang power in the neighborhood), or get beat up every day on the way to and from school. His introduction to the "Baby Bops" was simple enough: He had to choose a girlfriend from a line-up of willing girls—Mary, and a "big brother" from the "Big Bops"—Blacky. He received a tattoo on his right hand with the initials "BM," which he wears till this day. "I suppose I could have it removed," he says, "But I want to remember my past so I don't slide back down that road again. I'll always be a recovering addict; I don't want to ever forget that."

At eight years old he had sex with Mary—the "M," and sniffed glue all night. When he awoke from his fog the next day Mary was with another boy and he never was with her again, but the "M" on his hand stayed. Soon after that he had his official initiation where he had to fight the gang's "War Counselor"—the toughest guy in the gang. He got his nose broken, but he was officially a member of the "Baby Bops."—His new family.

Life was pretty good. He had new friends, plenty of women, the glue, and lots of cheap wine. Stealing, gang fights, glue sniffing, alcohol, and sex were pretty much his life for the next few years. "I saw lots of people getting mugged, stabbed, even killed," adds Julio, "That was just the way we lived."

He remembers stealing $100 bills from his father to pay for his glue. "You had to be 16 or older to buy the glue, so I'd give the money to a guy that was shooting Heroin in a basement where we used to hang out. He was in his thirties, or something. He'd bring me back the glue and he'd keep the change—the glue cost $3.00; it would keep me high for three days."

The orgies of glue were so intense, that after three days of sniffing, when he finally came to, his pants were soiled with urine and excrement; his throat coated with remnants of glue and vomit. "You dream you're eating, going to the bathroom, or whatever," he explains, "But you're really just lying there in your vomit and everything until you finally run out of glue."

When he was twelve his thirty-something glue buying buddy introduced him to Heroin for the first time. Julio remembers that he passed out and was sick for three days afterward. "When I woke up three days later I told my friends about it and they all thought I was cool. They wanted to know where I got the stuff so I took them down to the basement and we all got into it. Even though I didn't like it at first it made me feel special to have moved up to the next level—it made me a big man."

Soon, he was twelve-year-old Heroin addict. At sixteen he entered his first rehab program after getting busted while waiting in the car for one of his buddies who was making a drug score in an upstairs flat. It turns out the car was stolen and the police had made the plates. They threw him into detox for three days and then into prison at Rikers Island, NY.

Julio recalls: "I didn't know that in prison nobody does nothing for you just to be nice."

His twenty something, 6', 300-pound cellmate started doing favors for him—getting him cigarettes, sneakers and stuff. "Soon after he started putting his hands on me while I slept. He said I owed him for the favors. When I refused to do what he asked, he tried to rape me, so I cut him with some broken glass when I had the chance. He had his hands around my neck as we fought; the guards broke us up and put me in solitary. I ended up at Manhattan General for three months in a methadone program."

Unfortunately, Julio wasn't ready to end his addiction. "You've got to really want to be clean," he explains. "I kind of liked my life back then—I didn't want to change."

Julio recalls drinking the methadone and then shooting up; maximizing the effects of both drugs. Eventually, they threw him out of the program and back on the street.

His Dad sent him to Puerto Rico to live with his Mom because he couldn't deal with him anymore. Blessed with a musical talent, he met some guys who had a Rock 'n Roll band. "I became famous and well to do almost overnight," he says. "Even though I speak with an accent, I don't sing with one, and that was a very unusual thing."

He cut several records and appeared to have had it made, except for one thing; he was still an addict. When he was 21 he entered another rehab program and was clean for three years. In fact, he eventually became Director of the program. While he was there he got married and had two children. Even though he was off the Heroin he hadn't changed his outlook on drugs and alcohol—he still smoked marijuana and drank.

When he left the House of Rehabilitation he became a house manager for public buildings and fell back into his old lifestyle once again. Some of the tenants would give him free drugs for special favors on rent, etc. Eventually, his wife found out about his addiction when their kids were kicked out of private school for non-payment of tuition—Julio had spent all their money on drugs. He begged her not to leave him if he would get back into a rehab program. Three weeks after entering "Teen Challenge" a religious based program of prayer and counseling he received the divorce papers.

Julio is now 57. An addict for 20 years, he has now been clean of any mind altering substance for 26 years and is an Adult Counselor for The Center for Drug-free Living, a non-profit drug and alcohol treatment center in Orlando, Florida. After changing his belief system about drugs and his own potential he went back to school—he had dropped out in the sixth grade—and put himself through college, graduating from Empire State College in Rochester, NY at the top of his class. He founded Hogar Renacer, a drug rehab program for Hispanics in Rochester, and devotes much of his time to giving inspirational talks to youths on the dangers of drug addiction.

Julio has traveled to Nicaragua, Ecuador, Santo Domingo, and Venezuela sharing his powerful story for the benefit of others. He's been married to his second wife Rosa for twenty years and has an eighteen year old daughter, and a thirteen year old son.

I asked him why he has devoted his life to helping others overcome the addiction that has plagued him for the greater part of his life. His answer: "Every time I help someone turn his/her life around, I figure I've earned another year of drug-free living. An addict is never really over their addiction. I tell everyone I meet that I am a *recovering* addict. There are many days where I would like to shoot up again; I just tell myself I can't do it—the price is too high. When I see people come in off the street with tracks all over their arms, looking like death; it reminds me how easily I could be right back there again."

The scars on his wrists and across his chest—as well as Blacky's and Mary's initials on his right hand—are continual reminders of his former life. Julio explains: "When I cut myself like that I couldn't break the cycle of addiction, so I just wanted to die. I expected to get AIDS or hepatitis like a lot of my friends, but I was a lucky one. Like every junkie, I wanted to die of an overdose; At least that way if I died, I'd die high."

Among Julio's regrets are the damage he caused to his family and the prospects for his four sons who don't live with him—two from his first wife, and two from other former relationships. "I'm afraid they may take the same road I was on," he laments.

Julio knows that he can't change his past no matter how much he would like to. He talks emotionally of how people need to get the right belief system for themselves. He is focused on a future of helping others to get clean. I can honestly say that Julio is an inspiration to me. How many of us would use the excuse of a childhood like his as a reason for failure on any level. On behalf of the many people who Julio has helped to break the vicious cycle of drug addiction, and all those kids he may have prevented from ever starting; I would like to say, "Thanks, Julio; we're very glad you're still with us."

Steve is a homeless man that I met while driving around Orlando. He was holding a sign that read "Stranded, Homeless, Hungry." I am sure you have seen people like this on street corners or park benches where you live. There is a stereotype that they are all alcoholics or drug addicts. Instead of giving him money, I stopped and offered to give Steve a lift to a nearby restaurant. He refused, saying that he doesn't get in people's cars. I told him that I would meet him at a restaurant down the street a couple of blocks. I won't bore you with all the details that Steve shared with me. I am sure that some homeless people are in a situation that is over their heads and are looking for a solution to get back on their feet. I will tell you that in Steve's case the stereotype was true. He blamed everyone for his condition. Said the world was going to end in a year. He knew this to be true because of all the blacks (he used a term that I won't use) with white women. "Im not prejudiced, but it aint right" he said. He admitted to living on the street for 20 years and to being an alcoholic. He said his dad was an alcoholic, too, whom he hadn't seen in 20 years. Didn't know whether he was still alive. Steve had spent five years in prison for armed robbery. He carried with him a six pack of beer in a brown bag. I asked him how he got "stranded" in Orlando and he couldn't really answer, but mumbled something how his tent was stolen in Tampa. I asked him how he ended up on the street. He said his old lady (not his words) took everything he had. He met her when she was 15 and she got pregnant. I asked him what dreams he had when he was a young man. He said he always wanted to be a tramp so nobody could tell him what to do. It was clear to me that Steve was not happy to be answering these questions. He complained about the food and said he didn't like chicken, though I had met him at a Boston Market which had pretty much anything you wanted. He had ordered the chicken. I am sure that he would have been much happier if I had just given him money so he could buy more alcohol. As I recall, he didn't thank me for the lunch.

Your assignment for today is to contrast the two biographies you've just read. What have you learned from these that can benefit you in your search for personal growth? What personal beliefs were beneficial for each of them? Were self destructive for them? Was selfishness a factor in any of their stories? Was selflessness a factor in any of their stories?

What action can you take today that will utilize this in a positive way for your personal growth and for the benefit of others?

CHAPTER THIRTY

SUMMARY AND CONCLUSION

Congratulations. We've come a long way together—you and I—haven't we? You truly are an exceptional person. By now you believe me when I tell you that, don't you? Statistics show that less than one out of ten people ever invest in a process of self-improvement; and out of those only a third or so ever finish the program. It's too easy and comfortable to simply stay the way they are—even though they really don't like where they are. You are different, though. You knew from the start that you were meant for much more than the ordinary. You were aware that your potential greatness in so many areas of your life was just waiting there for you, like a treasure waiting to be discovered.

Your thought processes have been greatly modified over the last thirty days or so—some of that without you even being aware of it. You now look at yourself and your world in a much-improved way than before. You like and love yourself; and because of that you like and love others, too. You make new friends more easily than you may have ever believed was possible. You have a confidence in yourself that is contagious. Others like to be around you because you are a positive person. And, you are fun. You're fun because you enjoy life.

Isn't it truly exciting and wonderful to be able to find the positives in life where so many others only seem to trip over the negatives that seem to find them in every situation? Because of this you're able to experience positive emotions in every aspect of your life.

You're a better wife, husband, mother, father, friend, partner, or companion than you ever were before because you like and love yourself. You've learned to trust yourself, as well. This too is exciting, because you surprise yourself regularly with fresh and new ideas; and you take action on them for the benefit of others and yourself. Life is fun for you because you have clear goals—clear direction, and with it the promise of positive and beneficial outcomes.

Where others seem to be going around in circles—not having a clear idea of what they want, or even where they should be going, you know exactly what you want and you've created an action plan to take you there along the straightest road. You know that the shortest distance between two points is a straight line and that's the road you're on. Your goals—the life that used to be only a dream for you—are well on their way to being reached. Some of them may have already come true for you.

I'm excited and happy for you. Did I mention that you deserve these positive things? Winners always pay a price in order to achieve their success. You have proven to yourself that you are willing to pay that price in order to achieve the dreams you have identified for your life. Because you're willing to pay that price you can't fail.

You've taken responsibility for every aspect of your life. This has given you a peace of mind that most only dream of—but never achieve. You've trained your mind to not only think positive thoughts, but also to ask yourself the right questions all day long. This brings forth even more positive emotions, which continue to blossom into more and more creativity and happiness for you each day.

You've learned to forgive others and yourself easily for their mistakes. You know that to do otherwise accomplishes nothing; only to inflict more unnecessary pain on yourself. You've learned to build bridges every day instead of tearing them down. You've learned to live in and enjoy the present—the gift—while planning and expecting a positive and rewarding future for yourself and the ones you care about. Life is good, isn't it?

I want you to stay on the right road to your positive future. I know that you want that as well. Don't let the naysayers slow you down; or force you on a detour that you didn't plan for. Continue your investment in yourself by submersing yourself into a feeding program of positive material. Consult the list of source material at the end of this book. Many people that I know who have pursued a course like yours replenish their well of positive inspiration continually by listening to audio books, tapes or CD's while in their cars, riding their bikes, exercising, or gardening. Zig Ziglar calls this "The four-wheeled University." You've learned that the world we live in isn't generally very positive. You have to continually look for the positives. See if you can complete the following sentence. Birds of a feather, _____.

Birds of a feather flock together. Isn't this just another way of saying that you instinctively spend time with those who think and act like you do? Ducks don't fly with pigeons. Geese don't fly with ducks. Do you want to soar with the eagles, or scrap with the seagulls? You've made some dramatic changes in your thought processes and in your life. But, if you rub elbows on a regular basis with those who think negatively and those who don't share your vision you can easily fall back into the negative habit patterns that will do nothing but drag you down. It may be necessary for you to develop new relationships with those who think like you do.

In the days ahead you will want to keep reminding yourself of your goals. Re-reading and even re-writing them will keep your mind focused on the road ahead keeping you headed in the direction you have chosen for your life. I would also recommend that you make an appointment with yourself to re-read this book thirty days from now. Since you've already gone through the exercises you can just read it as a reminder if you like. You will pick up things that you completely missed the first time through. Of course, it wouldn't hurt to re-do the exercises that seem appropriate. You can read at what ever pace seems comfortable for you as a form of review.

I'd like to end with a review of the beliefs that you have now adopted as your own. Your "Perfect Ten" beliefs.

1. I am a winner (Or, I only fail when I quit trying)
2. I strive for continuous self-improvement
3. I like and love people and therefore people like and love me in return
4. I make new friends easily
5. I am worthy of the love and respect of myself and others
6. I am worthy of all the good things life can give
7. I am a person of action
8. I love my life and live every day with passion
9. I have unique gifts and abilities that can greatly benefit others and myself

10. I am responsible for every event in my life and I therefore am in control of my life

Don't forget to say these out loud each day with conviction and belief. Congratulations for being the person you are. Thanks, and goodbye.

PROLOGUE – WHAT NOW?

There's an old saying you may have heard; "There are no atheists in a foxhole!" I've recently heard it said somewhat differently. After interviewing survivors of Hurricanes Hugo, Andrew, Katrina and other catastrophes, there was one thing that everyone seemed to have in common. While the people hunkered down wherever they could find any shelter as the storms wailed with 100+ mph winds nobody was practicing "Positive Thinking." What do you think they were doing? If you guessed praying, you were right. We may not want to admit it while things in our lives are going fairly well, but when things turn very ugly most everyone wants to turn to a "Higher Power." Whether you want to call this higher power, God, Jehovah, Allah, or whatever, the fact remains that the concept of a being/beings with power and authority greater than us can be traced back to the beginnings of recorded history. Many believe that mankind has an inherent need to worship. The earliest cave drawings indicate our ancestors' belief in a supernatural force. The Egyptians worshipped multiple deities, as did the Romans. The American Indians worshipped the wonderful forces of what we would call Nature. Hindus worship literally millions of gods.

We have spent many hours through the pages of this book working on ways to reach our maximum potential as human beings. Like it or not, no matter how wonderful a job you and I do in becoming the best that we can be, our time on this earth as we are today is very short. Most of us will enjoy but 70 or so years. The Bible says "three score and ten," with special mightiness affording but a few years more than that. You've no doubt heard it said that death is a part of life. I can tell you from firsthand experience—I know you'll agree if you've lost loved ones yourself—that is small comfort when someone you love dies.

If you have ever been seriously ill, you know that no matter how positively you try to look at the experience the bottom line is you wish you were healthy again. It's very difficult to enjoy life when you're not feeling well. And while it is possible to overcome some health problems by the right mental states it is also true that the most positive thinkers get sick and ultimately die.

I'm assuming you have made it through this entire book with me and didn't just skip to this Prologue. You know that I believe each one of us has the right and even the obligation to get the most out of our lives for the benefit of others and ourselves. You've read these words many times by now in these pages. But is that all there is? I personally believe that there is more than just this present life of ours. I encourage you to further your personal development with other fine authors such as those in the Bibliography of this book. I also encourage you to look beyond "Self Help" genre books and tapes and begin an earnest quest to find the truth of why mankind is here, and what future awaits all of us after our present lives are over. I wish you the best in your quest for this truth. May your future in this life and whatever comes after be the best it can be. Thanks for reading.

Please further your submersion into positive material by subscribing to our website at www.fearisthemindkiller.net

As you know, you, the reader, are responsible for your life. Any outcomes perceived as being the result of reading or doing the exercises in this book are your responsibility alone, not the responsibility of the author or his agents. The author makes no guarantees and accepts no liability and wants no credit for any of your successes and/or failures. It is our sincere wish that all your outcomes be favorable and all your efforts be successful.

BIBLIOGRAPHY

The Encyclopedia of Phobias, Fears, and Anxieties -Ronald M. Doctor, Ph.D. & Ada Kahn

Anxiety and Panic Attacks, their cause and cure by Robert Handly, with Pauline Neff

Is it worth dying for? By Dr. Robert S Eliot and Dennis L. Breo Marion Merrell Dow Inc.

Triumph over fear by Jerilyn Ross

Dune by Frank Herbert

Unlimited Power Anthony Robbins-Simon and Schuster

Personal Power II Anthony Robbins-Guthy Renker Corporation

Jim Rohn-The Art of Exceptional Living Nightingale Conant

Zig Ziglar

The 7 Habits of Highly Effective People Stephen Covey-Simon and Schuster

Stephen Covey-First Things First Nightingale Conant

Neuro-Linguistic Programming Volume 1 -Dilts, Grinder, Bandler, DeLozier Meta Publications

Be the Person You Want to be -John Emerick Jr. Prima Publishing

Influencing Integrity -Genie Laborde Syntony Publishing

Peter Lowe's Success Talk

Mega Speed Reading- Howard Stephen Berg and Kevin Trudeau

Managing Transitions William Bridges Addison-Wesley Publishing Co.

Managing For Success by Karr & Associates

The Psychology of Winning - Denis Waitley Nightingale Conant

Brian Tracy - The Psychology of Achievement Nightingale Conant

Managing Face to Face Selling Skills -The Forum Corporation

Forced Focus-Marc Stephen Garrison

Jack Canfield - How to Build High Self Esteem Nightingale Conant

Relationship Selling by SGA, Inc.

SGA Interpersonal Style SGA, Inc

Managing Transitions-William Bridges'

Changing the Game-Larry Wilson with Hersch Wilson Simon and
   Schuster
Spin Selling by Neil Rackham McGraw-Hill Books
Alejandro and Associates
How to Win Customers and Keep Them for Life Michael LeBoeuf
   GP Putnam's Sons
How to Master the Art of Selling Tom Hopkins Warner Books
How I Raised Myself From Failure to Success in Selling Frank Bettger
   Prentice Hall Press
Getting To Yes Roger Fisher and Willliam Ury   Penguin Books
Sales Negotiation Skills That Sell Robert E. Kellar AMACOM
Consultative Selling Mack Hanan AMACOM
How To Read A Person Like A Book Gerald I. Nierenberg and Henry
   H. Calero Pocket Books
The Dilbert Principle Scott Adams HarperBusiness
Business Is Combat James D. Murphy Regan Books
Dogberts Management Handbook Scott Adams   HarperBusiness
Think and Grow Rich Napolean Hill
W. Clement Stone

Made in the USA
Middletown, DE
17 November 2018